Zoos and Animal Welfare

Other books in the Issues That Concern You series:

Zoos and Animal Welfare

Christine Van Tuyl, *Book Editor*

Christine Nasso, *Publisher*
Elizabeth Des Chenes, *Managing Editor*

GREENHAVEN PRESS
A part of Gale, Cengage Learning

GALE
CENGAGE Learning™

Detroit • New York • San Francisco • New Haven, Conn • Waterville, Maine • London

GALE
CENGAGE Learning

© 2008 Gale, a part of Cengage Learning

For more information, contact
Greenhaven Press
27500 Drake Rd.
Farmington Hills, MI 48331-3535
Or you can visit our Internet site at gale.cengage.com

LIBRARY OF CONGRESS CATALOGING-IN-PUBLICATION DATA
Zoos and animal welfare / Christine Van Tuyl, book editor.
p. cm. — (Issues that concern you)
Includes bibliographical references and index.
ISBN 978-0-7377-3818-6 (hardcover)
1. Zoo animals. 2. Zoos—Philosophy. 3. Animal welfare. 4. Animal rights.
I. Van Tuyl, Christine.
QL77.5.Z673 2009
590.73—dc22
2007036344

ISBN-10: 0-7377-3818-9

Printed in the United States of America
4 5 6 7 12 11 10 09

CONTENTS

Zoos have evolved over time from symbols of power and prestige of the early rulers, to institutions for education and research, to powerful businesses, and ultimately to a beacon of hope in a world facing alarming rates of extinction. Yet to some, zoos have always been and continue to be prisons where otherwise healthy animals waste away inside depressing enclosures, facing a lifetime of neglect. These critics will need a lot of convincing to believe that zoos can be beneficial to animals. People can learn more about the fears of critics and the future of zoos by tracing their evolution over time.

History of Zoos

Wild animals have been displayed in captivity for thousands of years. According to most sources the first known zoos were large collections of animals assembled in Egypt around 2500 B.C. Exotic wild animals were captured on expeditions, then displayed in captivity by early rulers as symbols of wealth and power. In 1500 B.C. Queen Hatshepsut of Egypt built a zoo, and about five hundred years later the Chinese emperor Wen Wang constructed the Garden of Intelligence—an enormous zoo that sprawled over 1,500 acres (607ha). Later many smaller zoos were founded by rulers in northern Africa, India, and China to show off the strength and riches of the current regime.

Studies also show that the Romans kept wild animals in captivity and sent them into battle in bloody public spectacles. Lions, bears, elephants, and other creatures were forced to fight to the death in public arenas to the cheers and shouts of onlookers.

The birth of the modern zoo did not happen until 1828, when the London Zoo dedicated itself to the study of captive wildlife in London. The success of the London Zoo set off a wave of similar establishments, including the first zoological garden in

Melbourne, Australia, and the New York City Zoo. In 1889 the U.S. Congress established the National Zoo for the purpose of breeding native wildlife.

Zoos Today

Today there are more than four hundred professionally managed zoos across the globe. In addition, there are thousands of roadside menageries and petting zoos. Every year more than one hundred million people visit a zoo in the United States, generating millions of dollars of revenue. Studies show that 98 percent of Americans have visited a zoo at least once in their lifetime.

Most major zoos in the United States are accredited by the Association of Zoos and Aquariums (AZA.) The AZA is the driving force of zoo advancement and requires that all members adhere to strict animal care standards. In addition, all AZA-accredited zoos must pursue the tenets of education, research, and conservation. While many zoos of the past merely strived to be entertaining, today's zoos have evolved into a greater role, educating the public about different species of animals and enticing them to take part in conservation efforts.

Today's zoos certainly differ greatly in appearance from zoos of the past. Visitors to zoos can recognize major changes in zoo exhibits. For the most part, small concrete cages have evolved into large habitat enclosures more reminiscent of each animal's natural environment. The San Diego Zoo, for example, is a pioneer in building "cageless" exhibits and features many different animals and plants in the same exhibit that would be found side by side in nature, such as the zoo's simulated Asian rain forest, Tiger River. On the other side of the country, the Bronx Zoo's Congo Gorilla Rainforest sprawls over 6.5 acres (2.6ha) and grows thick with trees, bamboo, and other lush landscape. This exhibit is home to more than fifty-five wildlife species and twenty western lowland gorillas.

Some zoos have even made changes to the types of animals they will house in their exhibits. The Philadelphia Zoo, for example, has decided to close its elephant exhibit, as elephants are not suited for cooler climates, and the Bronx zoo is also phasing out its elephant exhibit.

Animal welfare advocates, however, argue that zoos will never be suitable homes for wild animals and keeping them in captivity is never in the animal's best interest. They claim that most zoo

Zoos help animals like the bald eagle get off the Endangered Species List.

animals still reside in outdated exhibits that are far smaller than their natural habitats, resulting in repetitive, stereotypical behaviors called "zoochosis," such as pacing, swinging, and rocking. Animal welfare advocates argue that this repetitive, apparently senseless behavior indicates neurosis or even insanity, and is caused by loneliness, frustration, stress, and psychological and habitat deprivation.

Zoos of Tomorrow

Most zoo experts contend that as plants and animals continue to die off at alarming rates, zoos will grow in importance as centers for conservation. Many zoo supporters argue that zoos are the only beacon of hope in the race against extinction. According to reports from the World Conservation Union, human activity threatens 99 percent of all species. Another study says that a quarter of the world's plant and vertebrate animal species will face extinction by 2050.

The zoo community already celebrates several conservation success stories, including the reemergence of the California condor, black-footed ferret, American alligator, grizzly bear, and wild bison. There are also success stories for the Guam rail, Przewalski's horse, scimitar-horned oryx, and Spix's macaw. Zoo supporters contend that many other species can be saved from extinction by captive breeding inside zoos.

Many animal welfare advocates, however, argue that conservation is just a guise to hide the real nature of zoos as profit-driven organizations. They note that animals bred in captivity are rarely returned to the wild, and worse yet, some animals are the nameless, faceless victims of the zoo "business" which often ends up with more animals than it can care for. Some of the "surplus" animals are killed by zoo management in "cullings," while others are sold to animal dealers, research laboratories, poorly managed roadside zoos, or canned hunting ranches.

Can animals live a happy and healthy life inside zoo walls, or should they live in the wild? Will zoos be able to transform themselves to respond humanely to global extinctions, or are zoos simply an idea whose time is gone? The potential consequences that zoos hold for the welfare of animals is one of the topics explored in this book. In the following excerpts from magazine articles, editorials, books, and other sources, the authors debate the merit of zoos and their evolving role in our world. This book also features several resources to help readers understand the controversy surrounding zoos and animal welfare, including organizations to contact, a list of additional articles and books on the subject, and a list of facts about the topic. The appendix "What You Should Know About Zoos and Animal Welfare" offers advice to help readers conduct their own research, form an opinion, and take action. With all these features, *Issues That Concern You: Zoos and Animal Welfare* is a great place to start researching this controversial and fascinating topic.

ONE

Animals Suffer in Captivity

The Captive Animals' Protection Society

Animals in zoos are forced to live in artificial, stressful, and boring conditions, according to the Captive Animals' Protection Society (CAPS), an organization that campaigns against keeping wild animals in captivity. Zoo enclosures rarely match each animal's natural environment, forcing species that would travel hundreds of miles a day in the wild into small enclosures. Many zoo animals are so bored and unhappy that they exhibit stereotypical behaviors including needless pacing, swaying, rocking, and self-mutilation. In addition, important social relationships between animals are destroyed as zoos trade or sell animals. According to the CAPS, wild animals need to live where they can exhibit natural behaviors—in the wild.

Worldwide there are probably more than 10,000 zoos, with hundreds of thousands of animals held captive.

Zoos are a relic of a bygone age—a Victorian concept which, as our knowledge of the animal kingdom grows, becomes even less palatable.

An increasing number of people are concerned about keeping wild animals captive. So zoos claim they are on a greater mission

The Captive Animals' Protection Society, "Sad Eyes and Empty Lives: The Reality of Zoos," www.captiveanimals.org, 2006. Reproduced by permission.

than simple entertainment: for conservation, education and research. Zoos now favour terms like 'wildlife park' or even 'sanctuary'.

The Captive Animals' Protection Society [CAPS] is totally opposed to the incarceration of animals and believes that zoos misinform rather than educate, and further, divert funds from positive conservation. Animals remain threatened or are even driven to extinction, whilst precious resources are drained away on expensive, high-profile breeding projects with no serious hope of success.

Sad Eyes and Empty Lives

In the wild, animals react to their surroundings, avoiding predators, seeking food and interacting with others of their species—doing what they have evolved for. Consequently, even what might seem 'larger' or 'better' enclosures may be completely impoverished in terms of the animals' real needs.

Frustration and boredom are commonplace amongst animals in zoos and can lead to obsessive and repetitive behaviours in the form of pacing, swaying, and even self-mutilation. This is known as stereotypic behaviour and such pointless, repetitive movements have also been noted in people with mental illnesses. With nothing to do, animals in zoos go out of their minds. Disturbed maternal behaviour may involve over-grooming and the rejection or killing of young.

Studies by Oxford University scientists found that lions in zoos spend 48% of their time pacing and 40% of elephants performed stereotypic behaviours.

Even diets are unnatural, with zebras in zoos becoming overweight as the grass they are given is higher in calories than the grasses of the African savannah. The resulting obesity can affect fertility.

CAPS have filmed adult gorillas in zoos repeatedly eating their own vomit. A gorilla biologist, who studied wild gorillas in Rwanda with the late Dian Fossey, told CAPS: "I have never seen wild gorillas perform R&R (regurgitate and re-ingest, as it's known in the zoo world, being such a well known by-product of captivity) and I have never spoken to anyone who has. In fact, I have never seen a wild gorilla vomit."

Some animals suffer such serious behavioural problems in zoos that they are given anti-depressants, tranquillisers and anti-psychotic drugs to control their behaviours.

Zoos often refer to the animals they confine as being 'ambassadors' of their species, but just what message does it give when we see animals in such unnatural conditions, displaying disturbed behaviours?

The Longest Life Sentence

Space in zoos rarely, if ever, matches the animals' natural range. Animals who would naturally roam for tens of miles a day tread the same few paces daily. Some of the fastest animals on earth live in pens so small that they could not gather pace to a trot, let alone full speed.

A study published by CAPS revealed that enclosures in UK [United Kingdom] zoos and safari parks are on average 100 times smaller than the minimum home range in the wild for the animals they contain.

Another study of zoos worldwide found that lions and other big cats have 18,000 times less space in zoos than in the wild, and that figure rises to one million times less space for captive polar bears.

For fifteen hours a day, many animals may be shut away in their night quarters with even less room to move.

Some zoo enclosures prevent the inmates from enjoying even their most basic behavioural repertoire including exercise and social interaction. Birds are virtually stripped of their most precious gift, flight, often able to do little more than flutter their wings. Consequently, birds in zoos are prone to arthritis and osteoporosis.

However, it is not just a matter of space, but also the quality of the environment.

Chimpanzees are our closest relatives in the animal kingdom, their intelligence is universally accepted, but they exchange the

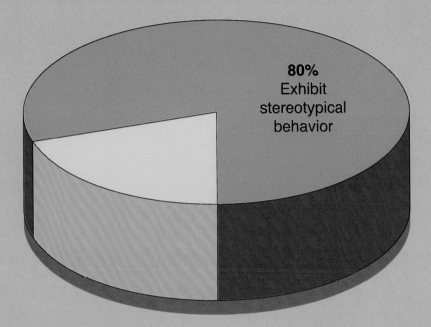

Percentage of Zoo Animals That Exhibit Stereotypical Behaviors

80%
Exhibit
stereotypical
behavior

Taken from: Zoo Check / Health Check, 2000.

infinite possibilities of the forest for little more than playground climbing frames which would not keep a human child occupied for hours, let alone years.

Reptiles need complex thermal ranges, variation in humidity, special phases of light and other factors that may seem difficult for us to appreciate as humans.

Zoos rarely have the numbers to match the natural social inter-action of herd animals. And when animals do find company, their world may be torn apart when cage mates are sold or become excess to requirements.

Solitary and shy animals are often in enclosures with viewing from all sides, and even a window in the night quarters as well. A study of gorillas in Belfast Zoo found that when there were more visitors the gorillas displayed "more behaviours suggestive of agitation, such as repetitive rocking, group-directed aggression and self-grooming.". . .

Animals bonding with their handlers in zoos is seen by some as a sign of the lack of activity animals experience in zoos.

Zoos Today

Zoos claim that seeing a live wild animal gives an unparalleled appreciation of the power and wonder of nature, but what are they really showing us?

TV wildlife programmes have ensured that our understanding of these animals extends beyond these pathetic exhibits. Indeed, CAPS believes school trips to zoos leave children with a distorted view of wildlife. A study of zoo visitor attitudes found that after people saw animals in zoo enclosures that were highly artificial they had "a significantly greater negativistic and dominionistic attitude to animals."

Signs on zoo enclosures can often give little information, or even incorrect details. A CAPS study of public aquaria in the UK found that 41% of the individual animals on display had no signs identifying their species—the most basic of information.

Studies have shown that most visitors spend less than three minutes looking at each exhibit, and sometimes as little as eight seconds.

We don't need to be wealthy to see animals in the wild. Wildlife is all around us, whether we live in a city or the countryside. From birds in the garden to badgers and deer in the woodland, we can all explore wildlife in its natural habitat with as little—or as much—effort as we want to put in.

Zoos claim that they afford people the opportunity to see something that many will never see in the wild. This is true; we will have to make do with books, magazines and television. However, can a few minutes of entertainment ever justify the tragedy of the disturbed behaviours and suffering we have outlined?

TWO

Animals Do Not Suffer in Captivity

The Philadelphia Zoo

Like most top zoos in the United States, the Philadelphia Zoo features state-of-the-art animal exhibits and cutting-edge health care. In addition to caring for the safety and physical well-being of its animals, the zoo also facilitates programs that nurture psychological health. According to the zoo's Web site, animals are placed in social environments that closely mimic their relationships in the wild, and they have opportunities to engage in many natural behaviors. The zoo also provides ample enrichment opportunities for exploration and novelty. The Philadelphia Zoo is one of the world's most renowned zoological societies and gardens, drawing more than 1.1 million visitors a year.

The health and wellbeing of the animals we care for are the Zoo's highest priorities. Our two full-time vets treat any ill or injured animals and carry out a Zoo-wide preventive medicine program. Our nutritionist designs diets that provide the proper nutrients and quantity of food for everything from a flamingo to a polar bear.

But our priorities and efforts don't end with the physical health of our charges. Of equal concern is the psychological wellbeing of our animals. Keepers and other staff devote much of their time to improving exhibits, procedures and programs that address these specific needs.

How do we do that? We have developed a range of programs that are generally grouped under the term "environmental enrichment," "behavioral enrichment" or just "enrichment." These programs focus on a variety of animal needs, which include companionship, feeling safe and secure, experiencing novelty and variety, and having opportunities to engage in natural behaviors. The Zoo's animal training program also supports our enrichment efforts, and we work closely with the greater zoo community as we continue to learn more.

Animal siblings playing in a zoo environment can help ensure their psychological as well as physical health.

Companionship

It's important to provide the right social environment for our animals. Many animals live in groups in the wild, and social interactions are an essential part of their lives. We always keep naturally social animals in groups at the Zoo to allow for that all-important interaction. Some species, like tigers, spend most of their time alone in the wild. These species are usually not kept in permanent pairs or groups, because there would be a high risk of fighting and injury.

Safety and Security

Providing the animals under our care with a sense of safety and security is vital to their psychological health. For example, we try to increase our animals' sense of safety by making sure that we design hiding places for those species that will use them. For animals that would normally escape from a predator by climbing a tree, we fashion tall exhibits so they can be well above the "dangerous" floor.

A positive relationship with their keepers is also very important to a sense of safety and security for the animals. Keepers use positive reinforcement, a quiet reassuring manner and simple "quality time" to establish and maintain positive relationships with the animals under their care. In a Zoo visit, you may see many examples of keepers interacting positively with the animals.

Novelty and Exploration

The Zoo provides animals with new experiences and a chance for exploration. Keepers achieve this by offering animals unfamiliar objects, new food items, changes in exhibit furnishings and unfamiliar scents, like spices or perfumes.

In addition to brand new items, keepers can use a range of familiar items to provide diversity on a day-to-day basis. For species like monkeys that eat a range of different food items in the wild, diet is a major area in which we focus on creating variety. So for these animals, we provide a large array of fruits and vegetables and change them from day to day. We're still learning about this

Speed Bump © 2004 Dave Coverly. Used with the permission of Dave Coverly and The Cartoonist Group.

area. For example, if an animal has apples and bananas in its diet, is it more "enriching" to get bananas but no apples for a week and then switch—more diet variety between days—or is it better to get both every day—more diet variety within a single day but less day-to-day variation?

Natural Behaviors

The Zoo gives animals opportunities to express their species-typical range of behaviors. Every kind of animal has its own repertoire of behaviors, and we want to make sure that the environments we provide give them the chance to perform those behaviors in a way that's as close to "natural" as possible. On an obvious level, this means that we give climbing animals the chance to climb and swimming animals the chance to swim. But sometimes, the goal is more subtle. For example, we need to make sure we design comfortable resting places that are right for each kind of animal, since most animals spend a lot of time resting.

We also try to make sure that we encourage animals to spend the "natural" amount of time doing each activity. Many animals spend a large part of their day in the wild looking for and gathering food. So at the Zoo, we often make food "harder" to find by scattering small food items in the grass or in a pile of hay or hiding food inside a cardboard box or paper bag. We also offer food items that are time-consuming to deal with, like a hard coconut or a leafy branch.

Training Program

Our animal training program is important to our overall enrichment efforts. Penguins voluntarily step on a scale so we can weigh them easily. Lemurs walk into portable kennels, making it easy and stress-free to move them if needed. A tiger allows a veterinarian to take a blood sample from her tail. At a subtle cue from his keeper, a gorilla opens his mouth so we can inspect his teeth.

Many of the benefits of these programs relate back to the enrichment goals. An animal that will enter a kennel voluntarily probably feels much safer than one that has to be actively caught and put in a kennel. The interactions create a more positive relationship between the animal and the keepers. And the opportunity to learn new cues and behaviors provides exciting variety and novelty for the animals.

Another benefit to the training program is that it gives animals under our care a greater degree of choice and more opportunities to control their environment. All participation in the training program is voluntary. If they do participate and respond "correctly," they are rewarded, typically with a small amount of a favorite food item. Research with some animals has shown that working for food is a rewarding activity and that an animal will keep performing behaviors to earn food rewards even if the same food is available "for free," sitting in a nearby dish.

Zoo Community

The Philadelphia Zoo along with the whole zoo community continues to learn more about animal psychological needs and effective ways of meeting them. The American Zoo and Aquarium Association (AZA) now considers active enrichment as part of basic animal care in zoos. The United States Department of Agriculture has required enrichment for primates in zoos for more than 10 years. There are a number of professional groups that focus on training and enrichment, including the Animal Behavior Management Alliance co-founded by the Philadelphia Zoo's assistant curator of primates and small mammals, Heidi Hellmuth.

THREE

Elephants Do Not Belong in Zoos

In Defense of Animals

Elephants should not be kept in zoos, according to In Defense of Animals (IDA), an international association dedicated to ending the exploitation and abuse of animals. In the wild, zoo elephants usually walk up to 30 miles (48km) a day, but in zoos, they are forced into small exhibits where they suffer from resulting painful joint disorders, foot infections, and digestive problems. Zoos are also ill equipped to regard elephants' fragile social relationships, trading elephants to other zoos on a whim, or tearing babies from their mothers at a young age. In addition, many zoo handlers still use sharp "bullhooks" to force elephants into submission. According to IDA, due to stress and health problems elephants suffer in zoos, most zoo elephants live only half as long as those in the wild.

Zoo officials work hard to convince the public that the elephants in their care are happy and healthy. On the contrary, most zoo visitors would be shocked to learn that many of the elephants on display survive on a daily diet of painkillers and anti-inflammatory medications to mask captivity-related ailments—the direct result of inactivity from confinement in artificial and restrictive zoo enclosures.

Restricted Movement Results in Health Problems and Premature Death

Zoos cannot provide the vast acreage necessary to accommodate elephants' need to walk. As the world's largest land mammal, elephants are designed for almost constant movement, and wild elephant herds easily travel over thirty miles a day on soft soil and varied terrains. Elephants in zoos, by contrast, spend their entire lives inactive in tiny enclosures, standing on concrete or hard compacted dirt. As a result, they suffer extremely painful arthritic and degenerative joint disorders and recurrent foot infections, as well as digestive problems. With all the stress and illness elephants suffer in zoos, it is no surprise that they live only about half as long as wild elephants. Elephants in the wild can live to be seventy years or older. According to the AZA [Association of Zoos and Aquariums], elephants in U.S. zoos die on average at thirty-four years old.

Many people believe that elephant enclosures are just too small to accommodate the migration patterns of the animal.

Psychological Deterioration

Neurotic behaviors are common consequences of severe confinement. Neurotic reactions can take the form of rocking or swaying, head nodding, and other repetitive motions. Sadly, many zoos still use force and dominance to manage elephants. Historically elephants have been managed through coercive force, such as chaining for prolonged periods and use of "bullhooks" and electrical hotshots. Chaining has a direct correlation to neurotic behavior in elephants.

The bullhook, also called an ankus, is a tool used to punish and control elephants. The handle is made of wood, metal, plastic, or fiberglass, and there is a sharp steel hook at one end. Both ends inflict damage. The trainer uses the hook to apply varying degrees of pressure to sensitive spots on the elephant's body, causing the elephant to move away from the source of discomfort. The thickness of an elephant's skin ranges from one inch across the back and hindquarters to paper-thin around the mouth and eyes, inside the ears, and at the anus. Their skin appears deceptively tough, but in reality it is so delicate that an elephant can feel the pain of an insect bite. A bullhook can easily inflict pain and injury on an elephant's sensitive skin. Trainers often embed the hook in the soft tissue behind the ears, inside the ear or mouth, in and around the anus, and in tender spots under the chin and around the feet.

Infant Mortality

Programs to breed elephants in captivity have largely failed, with high infant mortality rates and the premature shut down of most female elephants' reproductive systems. Without the complex social network that sustains elephants in the wild, new elephant mothers in captivity are ill-equipped to nurture infants causing many of them to die. Inexperienced mothers would normally learn from other females in the family herd, who help ensure the infant's survival. Zoos cannot begin to accommodate these vital social structures.

Elephants with Health Problems in U.S. Zoos

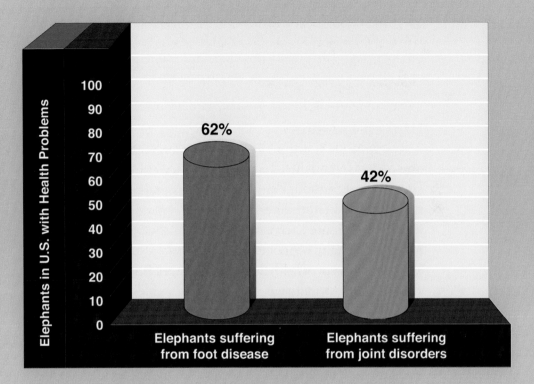

Elephants in U.S. with Health Problems

100
90
80
70
60
50
40
30
20
10
0

62%

42%

Elephants suffering from foot disease

Elephants suffering from joint disorders

Percentage of Elephant Pregnancies with Complications.

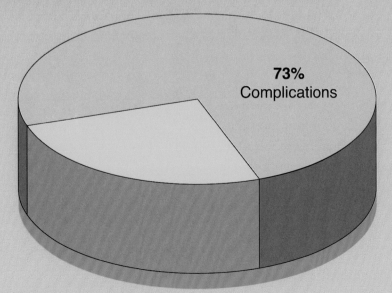

73%
Complications

Taken from: In Defense of Animals, 2006.

Incompatible Climates

Zoos in cold climates pose additional health threats to elephants, who originate from the warm, temperate regions of Africa and Asia. Cold winters force elephants indoors for months at a time, into cramped enclosures that are even smaller than their inadequate outdoor areas. Forced indoors, elephants stand on concrete surfaces in their own urine and feces, which can lead to foot infection.

Broken Families

Zoos simply are not suited to meeting elephants' social needs. In the wild, elephants live in complex societies made up of extended family members led by a mature matriarch. Female elephants stay with the herd their entire lives, and males do not leave the family until around fourteen years of age, always maintaining rich relationships with other bulls and females. In stark contrast, some elephants in zoos actually live in solitary confinement. Those elephants lucky enough to bond with another elephant in a zoo suffer when that friendship is disregarded by common zoo animal-swapping programs. Zoos shuffle elephants around like pieces of furniture with little to no regard for their feelings.

Devastation, Not Conservation

Zoos falsely claim that exhibiting elephants is part of a conservation effort to ensure the species' survival. In fact zoos actually contribute to the problem elephants face by abducting young elephants from their families in the wild to be put on display. True conservation involves protection of the natural habitat of elephants in Africa and Asia and strict anti-poaching efforts.

FOUR

Elephants Are Thriving in Zoos

The Association of Zoos and Aquariums

Today's elephants are happy and healthy in zoos, according to the Association of Zoos and Aquariums (AZA), a nonprofit organization dedicated to the advancement of zoos and aquariums in the areas of conservation, education, science, and research. According to the organization, elephants in AZA-accredited zoos exemplify excellent overall health and foot health. Many zoos have greatly expanded and upgraded their elephant exhibits, while others plan to do so in the near future. Furthermore, zoo elephants are in capable hands, as zoo elephant keepers average more than ten years of experience and exhibit outstanding knowledge of their charges. With more than two hundred accredited members, the AZA is North America's largest zoo organization.

Comments filed [in December 2006] by the Association of Zoos and Aquariums (AZA) with the United States Department of Agriculture (USDA) reveal new data that demonstrates elephants in accredited zoos are in very good health.

"Anti-zoo extremists should call off their orchestrated attacks against zoos. The facts are indisputable—elephants in accredited zoos are thriving," said AZA Executive Director Kristin Vehrs. "AZA-accredited zoos care for more than 280 elephants across

Health care is only one of the advantages elephants have when kept in a zoo.

North America. We have compelling data to show that AZA's mandatory Standards for Elephant Care and Management are working. The elephant population in AZA-accredited zoos is healthy."

Elephants in AZA-Accredited Zoos Are in Very Good Health

The AZA elephant survey results show, without any doubt, that the overall health and foot health of these elephants is excellent and that the AZA Elephant Standards for Management and Care are resulting in improvements to the care and condition of elephants in AZA-accredited institutions. On a 10-point scale, with

10 indicating the highest level of overall health, the average score for 284 elephants in AZA-accredited-institutions was 8.74.

Elephant Exhibits Are Improving

Over 40 AZA facilities have committed to expand and upgrade their facilities over the next 5 to 10 years to hold larger social groupings and focus on improved long-term reproductive success in the elephant population. Twenty-one AZA accredited zoos have significantly upgraded or completely rebuilt their elephant facilities in the last 10 years and three of these zoos built new facilities that brought elephants to their collections either for the first time or for the first time in more than ten years. Five AZA elephant holding institutions moved elephants out of their collections, primarily because they believed that they did not have the resources to commit to effective long-term elephant management.

AZA-Accredited Zoos Have Significant Elephant Expertise

The survey showed that the 78 AZA elephant holding facilities (out of a possible 80) that responded to the survey employ an average of 4.89 full-time equivalents (FTE) in elephant care staff totaling 382 FTEs. Each FTE represents an average of 11.3 years of experience working with elephants, which taken together represents over 3,880 years of current elephant expertise.

Public support for zoos is also strong. A recent Harris Interactive poll revealed that 95 percent of Americans said that seeing elephants in real life helps people appreciate elephants more and encourages people to learn more about them. That same poll showed that 85 percent thought zoo visits encourage people to donate money or time to conservation programs that help protect animals.

Elephant Conservation

AZA-accredited zoos are meeting the conservation test. When people visit an accredited zoo, they are supporting more than 85

Average Health Score for Elephants in AZA-Accredited Zoos

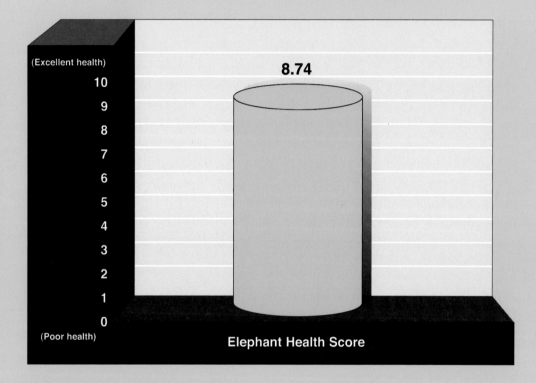

(Excellent health)

10
9
8
7
6
5
4
3
2
1
0

(Poor health)

8.74

Elephant Health Score

Public Support of Zoos

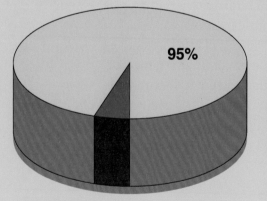

95%

Percentage of Americans who think seeing elephants in real life helps people appreciate zoos.

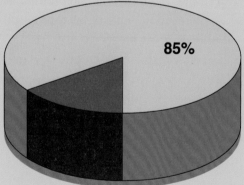

85%

Percentage of Americans who think zoo visits encourage donations.

Taken from: Association of Zoos and Aquariums, 2005.

elephant conservation projects in Asia and Africa, including field-based training, habitat restoration, reduction of human-elephant conflict and community-based initiatives.

"Based on the health of the animals, based on major investments in new facilities, based on the collective expertise of more than 1,000 dedicated professionals, and based on significant contributions to elephant conservation, AZA-accredited zoos are providing outstanding care for elephants," added Vehrs. "If extremist groups really care about elephants, they should join AZA in supporting elephant conservation in the wild."

Founded in 1924, the Association of Zoos and Aquariums (AZA) is a nonprofit organization dedicated to the advancement of zoos and aquariums in the areas of conservation, education, science, and recreation. Look for the AZA logo whenever you visit a zoo or aquarium as your assurance that you are supporting a facility dedicated to providing excellent care for animals, a great experience for you, and a better future for all living things. With its more than 200 accredited members, the AZA is a leader in global wildlife conservation, and your link to helping animals in their native habitats.

FIVE

Elephants Are Better Off in Sanctuaries

The Elephant Sanctuary in Tennessee

Animal sanctuaries are far better suited for elephants than zoos, according to the Elephant Sanctuary in Tennessee, the nation's largest natural-habitat refuge for endangered elephants. Unlike zoos, elephant sanctuaries offer an abundance of space for the optimal levels of elephant health and activity. Sanctuaries also provide nurturing, permanent homes for elephants, unlike zoos, which transfer elephants to other locations, separating them from family members and dismantling their complex social relationships. Furthermore, standards for the Association of Zoos and Aquariums (AZA) are no indication of health and well-being, as they allow for elephants to be chained for up to twelve hours at a time. The Elephant Sanctuary in Tennessee utilizes more than 2,700 acres (1,093ha), where elephants are not required to perform or entertain for the public; instead, they are encouraged to live like elephants.

E lephants are physically vigorous, long-lived, intelligent mammals. Female elephants maintain the most complex and extensive social network of any mammal studied. The basic social unit is the cow/calf herd of 9 to 11 members. Female elephants never

The Elephant Sanctuary in Tennessee, "Zoo vs. Sanctuary," www.elephants.com, 2004. Reproduced by permission.

leave their family herd. In the absence of human predation and drought, wild elephants can expect to live to the age of 65 or so.

Most elephants in captivity, including AZA zoos, are held in unnaturally small groups of unrelated adults.

Most AZA elephants do not breed successfully. Those calves born in zoos face an uncertain future. Of 11 African elephant calves born in AZA zoos since 1998, only 3 were alive as of June 2003. Of 5 Asian elephants born in the 12 months preceding June 2003, 3 are already dead.

Although zoo elephants are free from drought and human predation, elephants in AZA zoos are usually dead by age 38.

If present trends continue, AZA experts predicts only 5 Asian zoo elephants will be alive in 2049.

Two elephants frolic in a nine-foot-deep pond at a sanctuary in Tennessee. The chief difference between zoos and animal sanctuaries is that in sanctuaries, the animals have more space to wander.

Space Matters

A female elephant herd's home range covers huge spaces through which it moves to forage and browse for food, minerals, and water and to seek social contact with related herds. Wild elephants walk for miles everyday yet require only about four hours of sleep a day.

AZA mandates 75 square meters of indoor space and 252 square meters of outside space for two elephants. In the wild, home ranges of female African elephant herds, for example, vary from 15 to 50 square kilometers.

Let's do the math: in the wild, a modest elephant home range is 15 square kilometers or 15,000,000 square meters (1 square kilometer equals 1,000,000 square meters). In comparison, AZA's acceptable barn space for two elephants is about 200,000 times smaller than the space elephants would chose for themselves. AZA's outside yard space is about 60,000 times smaller than the smallest known elephant home range.

Not surprisingly, AZA elephants suffer from arthritis, foot rot, and other orthopedic disabilities that often contribute to their early deaths.

The Sanctuary is not another kind of zoo. We exist to provide a nurturing, permanent home for elephants already caught up in the web of captivity. Breeding our elephants to produce young that will, in turn, face a lifetime in captivity with no hope of return to the wild has no place in the Sanctuary.

AZA Accreditation Is No Guarantor of Elephant Well-Being

AZA's standards do not recognize or protect the lifelong bond between elephant mothers and their female offspring, nor do they acknowledge or protect relationships that AZA's unrelated adult female elephants have forged among themselves in their urgent quest for satisfying social affiliation.

AZA's standards permit elephants to be chained in their barns for up to 12 hours every day, year round. The Sanctuary does not permit chaining.

AZA's standards allow keepers to hit elephants as "training." The Sanctuary believes that hitting an elephant is never justifiable.

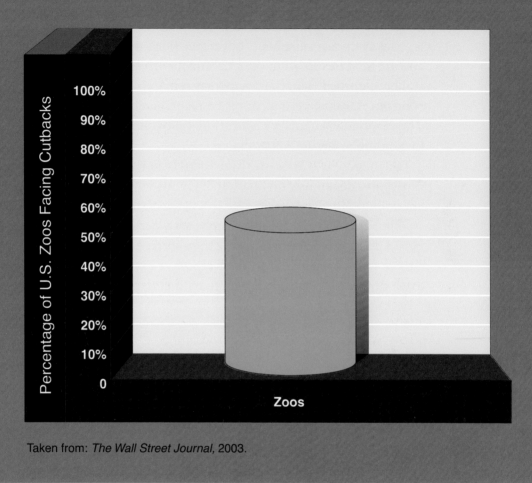

Taken from: *The Wall Street Journal*, 2003.

Elephants at the Sanctuary receive superior veterinary care from professionals whose experience and credentials meet or exceed AZA's standards. The Sanctuary, like AZA zoos, has written emergency protocols addressing safety and veterinary emergencies.

Safety for Animals and People

Since 1990, AZA has reported that elephants in their accredited institutions have seriously injured 27 keepers, 5 of them fatally.

The Sanctuary staff has never suffered a single serious injury or fatality.

AZA standards discourage but do not prohibit elephant rides and shows where the public comes into direct contact with the animals. Sanctuary elephants never give rides, never put on shows, and are never exposed to direct contact with visitors.

The Elephant Sanctuary supports research and conservation efforts in Asia and permits noninvasive research at the Sanctuary. The Elephant Sanctuary's educational programs for children and live online video are unparalleled.

Like many AZA zoos, the Sanctuary is a private not-for-profit institution depending on charitable giving and grants for its programming. . . .

The Sanctuary provides its elephants a permanent home in a large, natural environment where they are free to build lives they choose for themselves with the support of expert veterinarians, experienced staff, and loyal Sanctuary members.

SIX

Elephants Are Not Necessarily Better Off in Sanctuaries

Michael Hutchins and William Conway

Elephants do not necessarily enjoy a greater quality of life in animal sanctuaries as opposed to zoos, argue Michael Hutchins and William Conway, who work for the Association of Zoos and Aquariums (AZA) Department of Conservation and Science. While zoos are governed by strict AZA regulations, animal sanctuaries must only comply with the United States Department of Agriculture (USDA) standards, which are far less stringent. In addition, many sanctuary elephants are not allowed to breed, which, according to biologists, is important for social bonds. Finally, most animal sanctuaries have no long-term plans for income and revenue, which jeopardizes their ability to provide a healthy quality of life for their wards. Ultimately, despite the fact that many animal sanctuaries provide more space, bigger does not necessarily mean better.

AZA [Association of Zoos and Aquariums] institutions constantly review the status of their animal collections and facilities and it is every director's prerogative to determine which animals are appropriate for their facility at any given time and which are not. However, a common thread running through many of the media reports and in quotes from animal activists is that elephants would be "better off" living in these sanctuaries than in any AZA accredited zoo. This implies that the quality of animal care at these sanctuaries is better than it is at accredited zoos. It also implies that, within their respective categories, sanctuaries and zoos are all of similar quality. But is this really true? Absolutely not! . . .

Bigger, Not Better

[Many] elephant sanctuaries . . . offer hundreds of acres of space through which elephants can roam. In contrast, elephants at some urban zoos are maintained in considerably smaller areas (one acre or less) and therefore have little opportunity for exercise or social benefits that come from larger group sizes. However, this is changing. While many AZA facilities cannot offer the same amount of space as the two sanctuaries in question [in Hohenwald, TN, and San Andreas, CA], they are still quite large and complex. There are also many zoos that have new elephant facilities in the works, some of which are multi-acre.

While space may be important for elephants, there are no scientific studies that can assist us in determining either the minimum or optimum amount of outdoor space required for captive elephants. It is important to note, however, that bigger does not always imply better. There are many other factors that must be considered, including enclosure complexity and environmental enrichment, group size and composition, training, safety, veterinary care, nutrition, and so forth, when evaluating the quality of any elephant management program.

Lack of Breeding

Elephant sanctuaries typically do not breed animals or transfer them to other facilities for the purposes of genetic management. Most animals going to sanctuaries are on a one-way trip and will remain there for the rest of their lives. This is consistent with a sanctuary's sole focus on individual animal welfare.

In contrast, the focus of AZA and its members is both on the welfare of individuals and the population as a whole, both in zoos

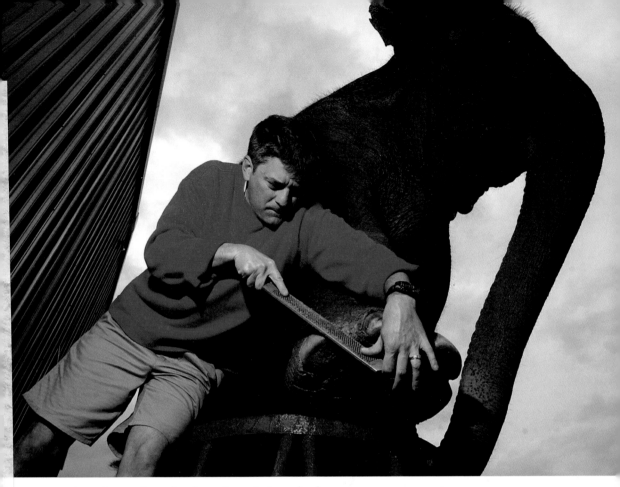

A trainer trims the foot of an Asian elephant at a sanctuary in Arkansas. Animal sanctuaries may not be better for animals due to less-stringent guidelines about how the animals are cared for.

and in nature. Participation in programs such as Species Survival Programs (SSP) may involve moving animals from one facility to another, either temporarily or permanently. In AZA zoos, elephants are seen as animal ambassadors, which play an important role in supporting conservation of their cousins in the wild. This is accomplished through a wide variety of activities, including public education, professional staff training, research, technology development, field conservation and fundraising.

Cooperative programs also control breeding so that populations do not overshoot their available space. Such programs are thus seen as contributing to professional and humane animal management and care, not detracting from them. Indeed, some biologists have argued that family life is critical to elephant social well-being. Births, such as those that recently occurred at Disney's Animal Kingdom and the San Diego Wild Animal Park, are known to have a profound effect on adult behavior, often further cementing female social bonds. Sanctuary elephants that are not allowed to breed will never have these opportunities, and this could be seen as diminishing their "welfare."

Standards of Accreditation

Although licensed by the United States Department of Agriculture's (USDA's) Animal and Plant Inspection Service (APHIS) and their state wildlife agencies, the elephant sanctuaries are not accredited by AZA. This means that they are not required to meet AZA accreditation standards, which are considerably more detailed and comprehensive than USDA standards. In addition, AZA established detailed Standards for Elephant Management and Care in 2001 and updated them in 2003. Nonmembers are not required to meet these standards, nor are they obligated to maintain them over time.

Of particular interest to AZA's Accreditation Commission is the long-term financial stability of a zoological institution. Without a predictable and reliable source of income, it is difficult or impossible for any organization to provide proper long-term care for animals or to ensure the safety of their staff. This is an especially important consideration for long-lived and potentially dangerous animals, such as elephants. Like sanctuaries, most AZA zoos are non-profit entities, but still have solid business plans to ensure that they are not solely dependent on unpredictable "soft money" donations. It is my opinion that sanctuaries, which are nearly totally dependent on soft money, should be required to submit pro forma annual operating expenses and projected revenue for the next 5–10 years before receiving any additional elephants.

The sanctuaries in question have their own accrediting body— The Association of Sanctuaries (TAOS). However, a review of the TAOS web site provided no information on the accreditation process or how long accreditation lasts. In addition, no information was available on the specific standards to which each TAOS member is to be measured against.

Do the sanctuaries in question meet AZA standards? The simple fact is that we do not know about the quality of animal care at these facilities because they are not accredited. This brings up a whole series of critical questions:

If additional elephants are added to the sanctuaries, will the facilities have sufficient staff to manage all of the animals appropriately and safely?

Are the keepers well trained and knowledgeable about elephant management? (AZA elephant program managers are required to

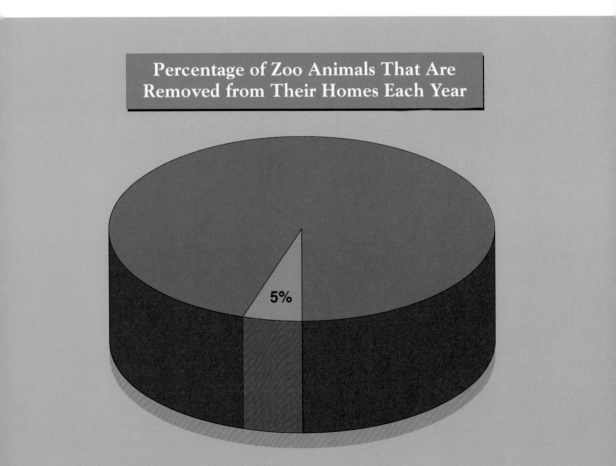

Percentage of Zoo Animals That Are Removed from Their Homes Each Year

5%

Taken from: Jesse Donahue and Erik Trump, *The Politics of 2005*. Northern Illinois University Press, 2006.

complete a certified Elephant Management course such as the one offered by the AZA Schools for Zoo and Aquarium Professionals).

Is the veterinary staff experienced with elephants, or with treatments of specific maladies that affect elephants, such as TB?

Are the care programs science-based? (e.g., one sanctuary's veterinary team includes an individual who prescribes "flower essences" and claims to communicate telepathically with animals).

What kinds of on-site veterinary facilities are in place?

Are there procedures to deal with emergencies or natural or human-caused disasters?

Can the elephants perform essential behaviors necessary for proper management?

Is the facility financially stable now and into the future?

These are all examined in great detail during the AZA accreditation process, as they should be at any prospective elephant holding facility. Why are answers to these questions important? There have been numerous cases where USDA licensed facilities, including so-called "sanctuaries", have degraded over time, on some occasions necessitating removal of animals and/or closure of the facility. Many animals have suffered as a result. . . .

Lingering Questions

Sanctuaries, like zoos, maintain animals in captivity, experience the same challenges of day-to-day animal management and care, need to engage in intensive fund-raising, and may support education and conservation.

Space seems to be the key difference between the sanctuaries in question and AZA-accredited zoos. How much space do captive elephants need for proper management? Unfortunately, there is little scientific evidence to help guide us in such decisions. Furthermore, it seems as if the media and public have seized on this single factor in their comparisons of sanctuaries and zoos. Chalk that up to good PR.

Zoos may find it difficult to compete with the perception of animals roaming "freely" through hundred-acre enclosures. However, I hope I made it clear that space is not the sole factor when evaluating the quality of an elephant management program. The difference between having four or one hundred acres may not be as critical to elephants as having social companionship, effective environmental enrichment and quality nutrition and veterinary care.

Until sanctuaries open themselves up for detailed peer-evaluation through periodic accreditation there will be no way to verify that their animal care programs, long-term financial stability, staff numbers and expertise, facilities, safety procedures and so forth meet professional standards. Nor will there be any way to ensure that such standards will be maintained over time.

It may be desirable for AZA members to cooperate with qualified sanctuaries. AZA has one accredited member sanctuary now and there could be more in the future. Although many AZA zoos maintain large numbers of geriatric animals and continue to provide them with quality care, it may be advantageous to have a place to send such individuals to live out the remainder of their lives.

The real question is: which elephant sanctuaries meet professional standards of animal management and care? The quality of care in non-AZA accredited facilities varies, sometimes widely. It is not enough for individual facilities to pass USDA inspections or to be "accredited" by TAOS, an organization that may be well intentioned, but currently has no detailed standards or method of enforcing them.

If the sanctuaries in question want to prove the quality and stability of their animal care programs, then I would encourage them to apply for AZA accreditation. Currently, there is no higher standard of professional animal care and these standards can be expected to continually evolve over time. Alternatively, USDA APHIS could adopt AZA's standards for elephant management and care and apply them to all elephant holding facilities as a condition of licensing.

SEVEN

Surplus Animals Are a Big Problem

People for the Ethical Treatment of Animals

Most zoos have a dirty little secret called "surplus animals," according to People for the Ethical Treatment of Animals (PETA). When zoo animals grow up and are no longer the cute, crowd-pleasing attractions they once were, they become a burden instead of a source of income for zoos. In other words, they become surplus animals. Surplus animals are frequently sold to canned hunting ranches, where hunters pay for the privilege of killing them. Often they are sold to other zoos of questionable quality, to live out the rest of their lives in neglect. Other times, they are simply killed by the zoo itself. According to PETA, surplus animals are a huge problem for zoos, and the situation stands to get worse before it can get better.

Despite their professed concern for animals, zoos can more accurately be described as "collections" of interesting "specimens" than actual havens or simulated habitats (real homes). Zoos teach people that it is acceptable to interfere with animals and keep them locked up in captivity where they are bored, cramped, lonely, deprived of all control over their lives, and far from their natural homes.

Virginia McKenna, who starred in the classic movie *Born Free* and received an Order of the British Empire in 2003 for her work in behalf of captive animals, says that her participation in *Born Free* made her realize that "wild animals belonged in the wild, not imprisoned in zoos. . . . Freedom is a precious concept, and wild animals suffer physically and mentally from the lack of freedom captivity imposes."

Cost-Cutting Hurts Animals

Zoos vary in size and quality—from drive-through parks to small roadside menageries with concrete slabs and iron bars. Although more than 135 million people visit zoos in the United States and Canada every year, most zoos operate at a loss and must find ways to cut costs or add gimmicks that will attract visitors. *The Wall Street Journal* reported that "nearly half of the country's zoos are facing cutbacks this year . . . [a]ttendance, meanwhile, is down about 3% nationwide."

Ultimately, animals are the ones who pay the price. Precious funds that should be used to provide more humane conditions for animals are often squandered on cosmetic improvements, such as landscaping or visitor centers, in order to draw visitors.

Animals suffer from more than neglect in some zoos. Rose-Tu, an elephant at the Oregon Zoo, suffered "176 gashes and cuts" inflicted by a zoo handler wielding a sharp metal rod. Another elephant, Sissy, was beaten with an ax handle at the El Paso Zoo.

The animals on exhibit are not the only ones who suffer. Most zoos have an area that the public never gets to see, where rabbits, rats, mice, baby chicks, and other animals are raised and killed to provide food for the animals on display. According to one zoo volunteer, killing methods include neck-breaking and "bonking," in which zookeepers place "feed" animals in plastic bags and slam their heads against a hard surface to induce fatal head injuries. . . .

Born Free, Sold Out

Zoos continue to capture animals from the wild to put them on public display. In 2003, the San Diego Wild Animal Park and Lowry Park Zoo captured 11 African elephants, a species designated as threatened, from their natural habitats in Swaziland. Experts, scientists, and researchers who study elephants in the wild strongly opposed the capture, stating, "Taking elephants from the wild is not only traumatic for them, it is also detrimental to their health. . . . [W]e believe the time has come to consider them as sentient beings and not as so much money on the hoof to be captured and sold and displayed for our own use."

Zoos are also pressuring the federal government to weaken the Endangered Species Act to make it easier for them to capture and import animals who are on the brink of extinction.

When Cute Little Babies Grow Up

Zoo babies are crowd-pleasers, but when they get older and attract fewer visitors, many are sold or killed by zoos. Deer, tigers, lions, and other animals who breed frequently are sometimes sold to "game" farms where hunters pay for the "privilege" of killing them; others are killed for their meat and/or hides. Other "surplus" animals may be sold to circuses or smaller, more poorly run zoos.

A chimpanzee named Edith is one example of a discarded zoo baby who fell into the wrong hands. Born in the 1960s at the Saint Louis Zoo, baby Edith was surely an adorable sight for visitors. But just after her third birthday, she was taken from her family and passed around to at least five different facilities, finally landing at a Texas roadside zoo called the Amarillo Wildlife Refuge (AWR). During an undercover investigation of AWR, PETA found Edith in a filthy, barren concrete pit. She was hairless and had been living on rotten produce and dog food. . . .

Another example involves Twiggs and Jeffrey, two giraffes born at the Cape May County Zoo. When they got older, they were sold by the zoo to a broker who subsequently sold them to a traveling circus. The director of the Cape May County Zoo actually admitted to seeing the animals' pitiful living conditions in the circus but did not have a problem with the situation.

Many animals in the wild have increased their numbers to the point where hunting is sometimes needed to keep the animal populations from starving.

Zoos across the country sold animals to the now-closed New Braunfels Zoo and continued to do so even after one of its owners "quit in disgust at the animal neglect." The director of an Arizona zoo sold several exotic goats to a dealer who was known to supply animals to trophy-hunting ranches.

Beyond Zoos

Ultimately, we will only save endangered species by preserving their habitats and combating the reasons why they are killed by people. Instead of supporting zoos, we should support groups like the International Primate Protection League, the Born Free Foundation, the African Wildlife Foundation, and other groups that work to preserve habitats. We should help nonprofit sanctuaries that are accredited by The Association of Sanctuaries, such as the Elephant Sanctuary and the Performing Animal Welfare Society. These sanctuaries rescue and care for exotic animals without selling or breeding them.

With all the informative television programming, our access to the Internet, and the relative ease of international travel, learning about or viewing animals in their natural habitats can be as simple as a flick of a switch or a hike up a mountain. The idea of keeping animals confined behind cage bars is obsolete.

EIGHT

Surplus Animals Are Being Dealt With

Jesse Donahue and Erik Trump

> Zoos understand that surplus animals are a problem, and they are actively taking steps to reduce the number of animals that are sold to private dealers and poorly run roadside zoos, according to Jesse Donahue and Erik Trump in their book *The Politics of Zoos*. According to the authors, the American Association of Zoological Parks and Aquariums (AAZPA) launched intensive investigations and generated a detailed report that estimated the number of animals that end up as "surplus." Ultimately, the AAZPA established guidelines designed to prohibit the sale of zoo animals to dealers who sell to canned hunting ranches and roadside zoos and also to ensure that other unwanted animals are euthanized in a safe and humane manner. According to the authors, these recommendations and guidelines ensure that individual animals are both cared for and respected. Jesse Donahue and Erik Trump are both associate professors of political science at Saginaw Valley State University.

The AZA [Association of Zoos and Aquariums] enjoyed legal and legislative successes during the 1990s, but it waged a much more difficult war internally and in the public relations arena over the continuing problem of how zoos disposed of their "surplus" animals. Zoos could proudly publicize their high standards of animal care, their conservation activities, and even their successful breeding of endangered species, but they preferred to keep silent about the fact that some of their unwanted animals ended up dead or in the hands of incompetent caretakers. Animal protectionists took every opportunity, however, to continue publicizing this kind of animal "abuse" by zoos. Worse, concerned zoo employees were going public about this dark side of the zoo, and the AZA membership itself was divided about how to deal with the issue. Slowly, the AZA developed a surplus animal policy, and by the end of the decade it had begun to build some public credibility by lending visible support to efforts to restrict the private ownership—and, by extension, abuse—of exotic pets.

Criticism of Zoos

As the decade opened, zoos again faced external and internal pressure to address the surplus animal issue. Animal rights groups began staging protests in front of zoos and aquariums and passing out leaflets to build public awareness about the surplus problem. The Friends of Animals, for example, sent the Oklahoma City Zoo a leaflet titled "Zeroing in on Zoos" that it distributed outside of the zoos it picketed. All of its arguments against zoos focused on the disposal of unwanted animals. The leaflet stated dramatically that "almost every major zoo in the country is either contributing to the problem or turning its back on it," and it alleged that even the prestigious San Diego Zoological Society sent a Dybowski's sika deer to a hunting ranch. In addition to confronting protesters at their gates, zoos also faced internal criticism from credible sources. In 1991, Donald Lindburg, the editor-in-chief of *Zoo Biology*, wrote an editorial critical of the zoo surplus animal problem, which Wagner distributed to the AAZPA board of directors. It became difficult for the AAZPA to ignore the fact that breeding programs were producing more animals than zoos could exhibit and that the surplus animals were sometimes being euthanized or sold to exotic animal dealers, eventually ending up in the hands of private owners, roadside zoos, or even hunting ranches. The AAZPA had tackled the surplus issue in the 1970s and again in the 1980s, but it appeared to be a problem with no easy solution.

Addressing the Problem

To address this growing problem, the AAZPA formed a surplus animal fact-finding committee in 1990. The committee's resulting report focused on the place of euthanasia in the dealing with unwanted animals. The report illustrated at least some of the AAZPA's understanding of when euthanasia should be employed, the uncertainty zoo members themselves felt about the issue, what they thought they should do about the problem, the trouble that zoos members had sympathizing with animal protection groups on the issue, and their strategy for managing the public relations difficulties that accompanied killing zoo animals.

The report confirmed that zoo animals were in fact ending up as pets or on hunting ranches. Using ISIS data (an animal registry system for zoos), the authors calculated the number of animals "removed" from zoos. Although their estimates were rough, because not all AAZPA accredited institutions participated in the ISIS system, they indicated that as many as 5 percent of all zoo animals were removed from their homes each year. Most of these animals went to other zoos, but the authors concluded that a significant number of animals ended up in the hands of private dealers and individuals. On the basis of their findings, they made suggestions for surplus animal guidelines that included increased education about the issue and an agreement between each zoo and those who took their animals. This agreement would control what happened to the animals in subsequent transactions by prohibiting the new owner from selling them to an inhumane research program, allowing them to be hunted, or selling them to people who were suspected of animal abuse. The report also offered recommendations about how zoos could keep most animals out of the hands of private citizens and hunting institutions: use birth control, separate the sexes, give the animals to another qualified zoo, sell to an accredited dealer, or give them to regulatory agencies for

A rare white tiger cub plays in a public display area. The American Association of Zoological Parks and Aquariums is working to ensure that surplus animals are not sold to canned hunting ranches and roadside attractions.

reintroduction. Although zoos hoped to send some animals back to the wild, the authors did not anticipate being able to do this often for "the next century or two." There were a few animals that fell into a "gray area" between pets and wildlife that the report indicated might be confidently sold back to the public through reputable animal dealers. As a last resort the report recommended using euthanasia, the most controversial method of animal disposal.

Euthanasia for Surplus Animals

The report suggested conditions under which euthanasia might be employed. Notably absent was the condition of an aggressive temperament as had been the case for one of the Detroit Zoo's Siberian tigers. Instead, the recommendations centered on poor health and population management. For example, the report approved of euthanasia in the cases where "animals receiving medical attention do not respond to treatment," "animals cannot carry out minimal biological functions," or "animals [have] no realistic chance of survival." At the same time, it reminded its readers that a commitment to saving species required preserving the gene pools, which had to be "managed" so that the surplus animals whose genes were redundant did not "deprive" other animals of a place on the "captive-ark." At least some of these euthanized animals might make appropriate food for other animals in the facility.

The internal political problem, the report acknowledged, was that not everyone within a given zoo supported euthanasia. The report noted that, because zoo keepers often developed an "emotional rapport" with the individual animals for which they cared, they were particularly reluctant to approve of euthanasia. The report noted that keepers agreed with euthanasia in theory as a means to "manage genetic diversity," but they often objected to it in practice. As a result, the report recommended educating both keepers and volunteers whose "sentimental involvement may be even more of a motivation" for their job. As the Detroit tiger case showed, unhappy zoo employees were more than a hypothetical possibility.

In addition to identifying problems with zoos' own employees, the report detailed the public's substantial resistance to euthanasia. Zoos unintentionally heightened the public's emotional feelings about animals with their "adopt an animal" fund-raising programs in the 1980s that encouraged citizens to believe that they owned a particular animal. Thus, the report recommended doing away with these programs, "de-emphasizing individual animals and . . . addressing species as a whole." Doing so would help the public, which the report described as "lack[ing] information and understanding of animals," accept euthanasia. Animal enthusiasts, the report continued, had "limited intellectual and ecological understanding of animals, with a very high humanistic attitude."

In addition to taking away animals' names and separating donors from animals, the report also recommended an elaborate plan to manage the potential public relations disaster lurking in every euthanasia decision. It advised careful documentation of why a particular animal was "surplus" through reference to its genetic redundancy. Following that, it suggested gathering keepers and other zoo professionals together for a meeting and handing out the AAZPA surplus guidelines and other reference materials on euthanasia. To head off criticism from public authorities such as city councils, which often had governing authority over the animals, the report recommended "stressing the risks of disposing . . . surplus animals to unqualified recipients and the negative long-range effects of excessive birth control upon the survival of endangered species." In short, the report recognized, as the judge in Detroit's tiger case had opined, that euthanasia decisions were ultimately political.

Conflicting Viewpoints on Surplus Animals

As public institutions, zoos would have to generate public understanding of their policies, yet the issues related to surplus animals remained contentious, even within the zoo community. These divisions were clearly visible at a 1993 AAZPA forum on surplus animals and hunting. On the one hand, some members resisted any accommodation on the issue, defending zoos' right to dispose of animals in any manner they saw fit, including sales to hunting ranches. One member noted that zoos were regulated by the USDA and wondered, "why should zoo animals be legally considered different from any other form of livestock?" A more moderate voice put the issue in the context of political attacks on zoos, arguing that zoos should "seek a position that would provide for a management policy based upon conservation principles, rather than . . . one which appears merely to serve the animal rights agenda." Speakers on this side expressed unease about maintaining responsibility for animals once they left a zoo's gates. On the other hand, some members insisted that zoos should care about the fate of all animals, not just those in their immediate care. The antihunting faction within the AAZPA argued that the AAZPA's philosophical support for the sustainable harvesting of natural resources did not include "taking a zoo-raised animal, putting it in a crate and allowing someone to shoot it as it is released." Others reminded their fellow members that zoos gained little political benefit from supporting game ranches: "why does the AAZPA want to be associated with these people?". . .

Protecting the Animals

The AAZPA board ultimately came down on the side of those members who wanted to protect individual animals. In its policy statement about the disposition of animals to hunting organizations, it reminded its members that zoo animals are "held in public trust" by largely public, taxpayer-supported institutions and that the public certainly did not imagine that its zoos were breeding animals for big-game hunters. Though they noted that some conservation policy involved culling, they stated that sending wildlife to hunting ranches impugned the role of zoos "as sensitive guardians and conservators." Just as zoos' public status guaranteed them some legal protections, it also obligated them to be at least somewhat responsive to popular opinion.

Ultimately the AAZPA was able to resolve the surplus issue as it related to hunting ranches and embarked on a campaign with animal protection groups aimed at curtailing exotic pet ownership.

NINE

Zoos Play a Key Role in Education

Wildlife Conservation Society

Zoos play a key role in education, according to the Wildlife Conservation Society, an organization that saves wildlife worldwide. In conjunction with the Bronx Zoo, the Wildlife Conservation Society implements education initiatives serving teachers, students, and the general public. With distance learning programs, science education activities, hands-on learning opportunities, and outreach campaigns, the organization strives to teach the importance of zoo life. The Wildlife Conservation Society aims to save wildlife through science, global conservation, education, and the management of the world's largest system of urban wildlife parks led by the flagship Bronx Zoo.

Education has been a cardinal tenet of the WCS [Wildlife Conservation Society] mission since its inception in 1895. Today, the Education Division supports the science literacy of teachers nationwide, bolstering the capacity of international environmental educators on several continents, and enhancing the eco-literacy of families and children in the boroughs of New York City and the tri-state area. By raising conservation awareness and providing tools for conservation action, the Education Division is preparing the next generation of conservation educators and action-oriented citizens. . . .

Zoos Teach from a Distance

During the past five years, the WCS Education Division has created a stellar interactive videoconference program for school classrooms. Developed with funding from the U.S. Department of Education and Lucent Technologies Foundation, Distance Learning Expeditions uses . . . the Internet to bring live broadcasts to students from New York to California and from Mexico to Great Britain. Many of these students have no access to a zoo locally.

The Distance Learning Expeditions feature 50-minute videoconferences, as well as pre- and post-videoconference materials, to teach students about wildlife conservation and ecology. A "One WCS" exemplar, the program uses the organization's world-renowned scientific and environmental education resources. In addition, viewers have access via remote-controlled cameras to the Bronx Zoo's unparalleled collections of live animals, as well as its award-winning curricula and scientific field research. According to an independent evaluation, "In all measures of use and effectiveness, the Distance Learning Expeditions program is positively rated." During the past school year, the program provided videoconferences for nearly 8,000 students in 15 states, with 604 teachers participating.

Tori Howe, a student from Maine, said that she likes the fact that she doesn't have to leave the classroom to see the Zoo. Unlike a TV show or a Web site, "You can ask questions," she said. Jill Bell, her teacher, said that her students, "are accessing a primary source," despite the fact that the school is miles from the nearest zoo. . . .

Zoos and Science Education

Programming for city and area schools continues to be vital to the science education of thousands of elementary and high school students. There is growing consensus that quality programming during after-school hours prevents risky behavior and keeps kids safe. This year, City cultural institutions linked with Department of

Youth and Community Development out-of-school-time providers to collaborate in Cultural After-School Adventures (CASA). After school and on weekends, CASA programs offer City youth enriching, educational, and diverse experiences.

In the 2006 pilot CASA programs, education staff at Bronx Zoo, Prospect Park Zoo, and New York Aquarium designed programs about ecology and the importance of wildlife conservation. They trained staff at after-school centers to engage children in multidisciplinary environmental learning activities. These programs included visits to the zoos or aquarium and family participation days.

School visits to zoos can be influential in the future of zoos and the animals they help to protect.

In the highly successful Distance Learning Adventures, Bronx Zoo exhibits and animals are integrated into programming through the use of remote-controlled cameras and videoconferencing technology. Very popular with teachers across the country, these courses are constantly being revised and updated, and will soon feature live video feeds from the *Madagascar!* exhibit. . . .

Zoo Education and Conservation

Throughout the New York metro area, our parks provide abundant inspiration and staff expertise to communicate to the broad public the issues surrounding the decline of the wild. In part, lack of awareness of these issues stems from a problem only recently named by social psychologists: nature deficit syndrome. The disorder results from the overwhelming impact of technology and the imposition of the built environment, which push nature from our collective psyches. From strategic locations in four New York City boroughs, WCS education outreach overcomes the effects of this disorder by introducing young and old to environmental issues and inspiring action on behalf of threatened wildlife and habitats.

At Prospect Park Zoo, nearly 10,000 children and adult urban dwellers in Brooklyn were introduced to wildlife science in preschools, libraries, hospitals, women's shelters, after-school programs, and parks. Young audiences participated in an interactive puppet show that utilized movement, song, and visual aids to reinforce relevant developmental skills, such as shape recognition, while fostering a connection to animals. Other audiences and intergenerational groups used their observation and cooperation skills to hypothesize about animal form and function, and children with cognitive, physical, and visual disabilities took part in engaging educational experiences through the use of multisensory instructional methods.

The Wildlife Theater, based at the Central Park Zoo, provides outreach and conservation education for school-age children throughout the greater New York metropolitan area. Innovative programs added this year include Cool Rain Forest Connections, which highlights sustainable development. Audiences take away a better understanding of this complex concept and a new awareness about the direct relationship between small, personal acts of conservation and the survival of the rain forest.

Zoo Education and Outreach

Bronx Zoo instructors, teacher trainers, and volunteers provide enrichment programs to patients in hospitals and nursing homes, including the Carl Sagan Discovery Program at the Children's Hospital at Montefiore. The Queens Zoo Education outreach program engages in highly regarded experiences at community libraries, YMCAs, Boys and Girls Clubs, and senior centers. Onsite Discovery Centers at Queens and Prospect Park Zoos draw the public in to learn what a zoo vet does, "go camping" under the stars, get up-close to a tarantula, observe artifacts, and learn about New York wildlife.

International education initiatives build capacity for environmental education by providing professional training and curriculum materials to conservation educators worldwide. In August 2005, international trainers, the WCS Shanghai Office, and two former WCS/CV Starr Environmental Education Fellows provided workshops for 60 schoolteachers in Shanghai and Hunchun, China. In northeast China's Heilongjiang Province, Hunchun is the gateway to one of China's last remaining tiger habitats, so the children growing up in the region will be critical to the tiger's survival there. The Mandarin-language edition of WCS's *Teachers for Tigers* manual provides teachers and their students with activities to promote attitudes and behaviors supporting tiger conservation.

TEN

Zoos Do Not Play a Key Role in Education

Dale Jamieson

Zoos do not play a key role in education, according to Dale Jamieson, an author and zoo expert. Numerous studies illustrate that zoos have little—if any—educational effect on visitors, with zoo-goers displaying the same prejudices toward animals as the general public. Even more disturbing, some zoo patrons leave the zoo knowing less about animals than they did before their visit. In addition, Jamieson argues that zoos do little to facilitate useful and meaningful research. Overall, the educational and research benefits of zoos do not outweigh the negative repercussions of keeping animals in captivity.

There is a presumption against keeping wild animals in captivity. If this presumption is to be overcome, it must be shown that there are important benefits that can be obtained only by keeping animals in zoos.

What might some of these important benefits be? Four are commonly cited: amusement, education, opportunities for scientific research, and help in preserving species.

Dale Jamieson, from *In Defense of Animals*. New York, NY: Blackwell Publishers, 1985. Reproduced by permission of Blackwell Publishers.

Amusement and Education

Amusement was certainly an important reason for the establishment of the early zoos, and it remains an important function of contemporary zoos as well. Most people visit zoos in order to be entertained, and any zoo that wishes to remain financially sound must cater to this desire. Even highly regarded zoos have their share of dancing bears and trained birds of prey. But although providing amusement for people is viewed by the general public as a very important function of zoos, it is hard to see how providing such amusement could possibly justify keeping wild animals in captivity.

Most curators and administrators reject the idea that the primary purpose of zoos is to provide entertainment. Indeed, many agree that the pleasure we take in viewing wild animals is not in itself a good enough reason to keep them in captivity. Some curators see baby elephant walks, for example, as a necessary evil, or defend such amusements because of their role in educating people, especially children, about animals. It is sometimes said that people must be interested in what they are seeing if they are to be educated about it, and entertainments keep people interested, thus making education possible.

Studies Show Zoos Don't Educate

This brings us to a second reason for having zoos: their role in education. This reason has been cited as long as zoos have existed. For example, in its 1898 annual report, the New York Zoological Society resolved to take "measures to inform the public of the great decrease in animal life, to stimulate sentiment in favor of better protection, and to cooperate with other scientific bodies . . . [in] efforts calculated to secure the perpetual preservation of our higher vertebrates." Despite the pious platitudes that are often uttered about the educational efforts of zoos, there is little evidence that zoos are very successful in educating people about animals. Indeed, a literature review commissioned by the American Zoo and Aquarium Association (available on their website) concludes that "[l]ittle to no systematic research has been conducted on the impact of visits to zoos and aquariums on visitor conservation knowledge, awareness, affect, or behavior." The research that is available is not encouraging. Stephen Kellert has found that zoo-goers display the same prejudices about animals as the general public. He is quoted in *The New York Times* as saying that "[a] majority expressed willingness to eliminate whole classes of animals altogether, including mosquitoes, cockroaches, fleas, moths, and spiders." His studies have even indicated that people know less about animals after visiting a zoo than they did before. One reason why some zoos have not done a better job in educating people is that many of them make no real effort at education. In the case of others the problem is an apathetic and unappreciative public.

School field trips to the zoo may not be as educational as administrators would hope.

Edward G. Ludwig's (1981) study of the zoo in Buffalo, New York, revealed a surprising amount of dissatisfaction on the part of young, scientifically inclined zoo employees. Much of this dissatisfaction stemmed from the almost complete indifference of the public to the zoo's educational efforts. Ludwig's study indicated that most animals are viewed only briefly as people move quickly past cages. The typical zoo-goer stops only to watch baby animals or those who are begging, feeding, or making sounds. Ludwig reported that the most common expressions used to described animals are "cute," "funny-looking," "lazy," "dirty," "weird," and "strange." More recently, Frans de Waal has noted that after spending two or three minutes watching chimpanzees, zoo-goers often say as they walk away, "Oh, I could watch them for hours!"

Of course, it is undeniable that some education occurs in some zoos. But this very fact raises other issues. What is it that we want people to learn from visiting zoos? Facts about the physiology and behavior of various animals? Attitudes towards the survival of endangered species? Compassion for the fate of all animals? To what degree does education require keeping wild animals in captivity? Couldn't most of the educational benefits of zoos be obtained through videos, lectures, and computer simulations? Indeed, couldn't most of the important educational objectives better be achieved by exhibiting empty cages with explanations of why they are empty?

Fluff © 1998 Nina Paley. Used with the permission of Nina Paley and The Cartoonist Group.

Zoos and Research

A third reason for having zoos is that they support scientific research This, too, is a benefit that was pointed out long ago. Sir Humphrey Davy, one of the founders of the Zoological Society of London, wrote in 1825: "It would become Britain to offer another, and a very different series of exhibitions to the population of her metropolis; namely, animals brought from every part of the globe to be applied either to some useful purpose, or as objects of scientific research—not of vulgar admiration!" Zoos support scientific research in at least three ways: they fund field research by scientists not affiliated with zoos; they employ other scientists as members of zoo staffs; and they make otherwise inaccessible animals available for study.

We should note first that very few zoos support any real scientific research. Fewer still have staff scientists with full-time research appointments. Among those that do, it is common for their scientists to study animals in the wild rather than those in zoo collections. Much of this research, as well as other field research that is supported by zoos, could just as well be funded in a different way—say, by a government agency. The question of whether there should be zoos does not turn on the funding for field research which zoos currently provide. The significance of the research that is actually conducted in zoos is a more important consideration. . . .

A Question of Ethics

Finally, there is the goal of obtaining knowledge about animals for its own sake. Knowledge is certainly something which is good and, everything being equal, we should encourage people to seek it for its own sake. But everything is not equal in this case. There is a moral presumption against keeping animals in captivity. This presumption can be overcome only by demonstrating that there are important benefits that must be obtained in this way if they are to be obtained at all. It is clear that this is not the case with knowledge for its own sake. There are other channels for our intellectual curiosity, ones that do not exact such a high moral price. Although our quest for knowledge for its own sake is important, it is not important enough to overcome the moral presumption against keeping animals in captivity.

In assessing the significance of research as a reason for having zoos, it is important to remember that very few zoos do any research at all. Whatever benefits result from zoo research could just as well be obtained by having a few zoos instead of the hundreds which now exist. The most this argument could establish is that we are justified in having a few very good zoos. It does not provide a defense of the vast majority of zoos which now exist.

ELEVEN

Captive Breeding Programs Contribute to Conservation

The Association of Zoos and Aquariums

Zoos play a major role in wildlife conservation, according to the Association of Zoos and Aquariums (AZA), the nation's largest nonprofit association for the advancement of zoos. AZA members have launched aggressive conservation efforts with much success—sometimes saving species from the brink of extinction. According to the AZA, in 2006 conservation campaigns resulted in a promising future for dozens of species. Elephants, swans, antelopes, manatees, and turtles are just some of the types of animals enjoying a renewed chance for survival due to the efforts of AZA-accredited zoos and organizations nationwide.

The Association of Zoos and Aquariums (AZA) . . . announced its top 10 wildlife conservation success stories for 2006. From elephants to amphibians, AZA-accredited zoos and aquariums spearheaded new efforts to protect wild animals—in some cases bringing them back from the brink of extinction.

"When people come to an accredited zoo or aquarium, they are not only getting a safe, fun family experience, they are participating in a global effort to save wildlife. We are linking the animals you see in AZA-accredited zoos and aquariums to significant wild animal conservation programs," said AZA President and CEO Jim

Maddy. "Zoos and aquariums are changing the way people think about their role in conservation through an up-close connection to the natural world."

Elephant Vasectomies

While poaching and habitat loss are causing elephant populations to decline worldwide, wildlife officials are culling elephants in confined areas, such as South Africa's Kruger National Park, where elephants are dangerously overpopulated. Culling can distress the communities of these highly social animals. Offering a safe and effective solution, a team of experts from Disney's Animal Kingdom and San Diego Zoo's Wild Animal Park developed a procedure for population control—elephant vasectomies. The technical team trained several African veterinarians how to do the procedure, and researchers hope it will help advance techniques for surgery on other large animals, including hippos and rhinoceros. . . .

Bringing Back the American Burying Beetle

The American burying beetle was listed as endangered by the US Fish and Wildlife Service [USFWS] in 1989 and in 2006 became the first insect ever to be managed by an AZA Species Survival Plan. These beetles are important scavengers in their ecosystem, eating decaying carcasses and burying them in order to lay their eggs. Thanks to AZA-accredited institutions like Roger Williams Park Zoo and Saint Louis Zoo working together with the USFWS, new populations are being reintroduced and established in multiple areas.

Bongos are Back

The bongo, a threatened forest antelope native to Africa, is returning to its homeland thanks to a breeding program and public education efforts managed by the AZA Bongo Species Survival Plan and partner conservation organization, Mount Kenya Wildlife Conservancy. AZA zoos worked to establish a stable population of bongos in American zoos then released the animals back into the wild.

Black and white ruffed lemurs, once on the critically endangered list, are making a comeback due to conservation efforts in cooperation with zoos.

Sound the Trumpets

Two trumpeter swans bred and released into the wild by the Lincoln Park Zoo in Chicago have made history by hatching two healthy chicks. This is the first known wild trumpeter swan nesting in the state of Illinois since 1847.

Manatees and Turtles Rescued

AZA-accredited institutions along the East Coast of the United States are partnering to rescue and rehabilitate marine animals that are injured, sick or stranded and release them back into the wild. Threatened species, such as manatees, and endangered species, including sea turtles, are rescued through these networks. SeaWorld Orlando and Lowry Park Zoo in Tampa, Fla., have been instrumental in rehabilitating and releasing over 475 manatees—a significant contribution to the 3,100 manatees that currently reside in Florida waters. In addition, more than 20 AZA institutions, including South Carolina Aquarium and Riverbanks Zoo and Garden, are involved with sea turtle monitoring, rescue and rehabilitation.

Percentage of World's Mammals Threatened with Extinction

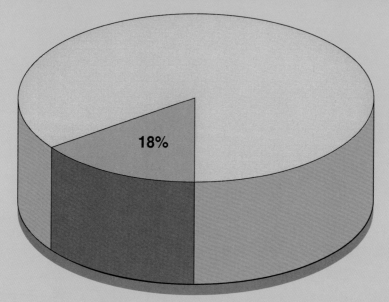

18%

Percentage of World's Birds Threatened with Extinction

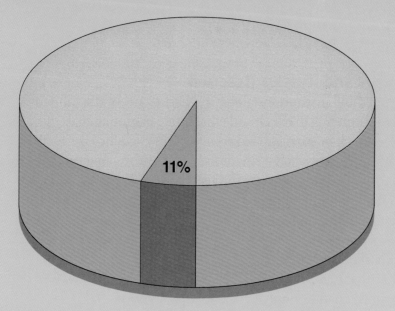

11%

Taken from: Jeffrey P. Bonner, *Sailing with Noah*. Missouri: University of Missouri Press.

Evading Extinction

AZA's Species Survival Plan (SSP) breeding programs were instrumental in saving the Guam rail, Attwater's prairie chicken, California condor and Micronesian kingfisher from extinction. Each of these bird species were essentially extinct in the wild; however, several AZA zoos took in pairs of the birds from the wild and breeding them, establishing a stable population, and reintroducing the birds back to the wild.

Breeding the Black-Footed Ferret

Twenty-five years ago, AZA-accredited zoos captured and bred the last remaining black-footed ferrets in an attempt to prevent their extinction. Today, the black-footed ferret population numbers approximately 1,000, of which more than half were reared in AZA institutions. Working alongside other AZA institutions, Cheyenne Mountain Zoo has led the charge in the Black-Footed Ferret Species Survival Plan. In 2006, 24 kits were born at the zoo, and seven have been sent to the U.S. Fish and Wildlife Service (USFWS) National Black-Footed Ferret Conservation Center in preparation for their release into the wild.

Saving the Frogs

Hundreds of frog, toad, salamander and other amphibian species are on the verge of extinction due to a devastating disease caused by the chytrid fungus. Scientists from the Smithsonian National Zoological Park played a large role in identifying the chytrid fungus as the culprit. Although individual frogs can be treated for chytrid, there is no way to remove it from the environment. To save frogs, AZA zoos and aquariums are collecting healthy pairs and bringing them into zoos to breed, creating a hedge against extinction.

Reintroducing the White-Winged Guan

The white-winged guan is a critically endangered bird native to the arid valleys of northwest Peru. Fewer than 200 individuals remain in the wild. The AZA Conservation Endowment Fund supported a project to increase the population and enhance community outreach at the Chaparri Community Ecological Reserve in Peru. Goals include establishing a population of 40 white-winged guans in the reserve by 2007 and educating local residents about the project.

Over the Rainbow, Palila Birds Fly

Seven palila, critically endangered honeycreepers native to Hawaii, were released into the wild in February 2006. They were released into the Puu Mali Forest Reserve on Mauna Kea. Twenty-two palila have been released into the reserve since 2003. The Maui Bird Conservation Center was established in 1996 as part of the Hawaiian Endangered Bird Conservation Program (HEBCP), which is part of the AZA-accredited San Diego Zoo's department of Conservation and Research for Endangered Species. The HEBCP is working to recover 22 endangered bird species in Hawaii. Other native Hawaiian species that are being propagated and managed at breeding centers, and which may soon become part of the release efforts, are the Maui parrotbill, Hawaii 'akepa and creeper, nene, and 'alala.

TWELVE

Captive Breeding Programs Are a Failure

Animal Rights Malta

Zoos do not contribute to conservation or species preservation with their captive breeding programs, according to Animal Rights Malta, an organization that supports animal rights and opposes zoos. According to Animal Rights Malta, there are many problems associated with captive breeding, such as the inbreeding that results when animals are bred with too small a gene pool. In addition, the inhumane nature of zoos does not contribute to natural animal behaviors such as breeding and instead results in neurotic and compulsive actions. Finally, few captive animals are ever successfully reintroduced into the wild, due to the problem of habitat restoration and the fact that few animals learn natural survival skills while held in captivity. Ultimately, the majority of animals in zoos are not endangered, nor do they stand a chance of returning to their natural habitats, according to the organization.

Zoos often claim that they are "arks", which can preserve species whose habitat has been destroyed, or which were wiped out in the wild for other reasons (such as hunting). They suggest that they can maintain the species in captivity until the cause of the creature's extirpation is remedied, and then successfully reintroduce the

Animal Rights Malta, "No Zoos in Malta: Here Are Some Facts About Zoos," www.animalrights malta.com, 2005. Reproduced by permission.

A loggerhead turtle is released into the Gulf of Mexico. Animals released back into their natural environment after being in captivity for a time may not survive the transition back to their natural habitat.

animals to the wild, resulting in a healthy, self-sustaining population. Zoos often defend their existence against challenges from the AR [Animal Rights] movement on these grounds.

Problems with Captive Breeding

There are several problems with this argument, however. First, the number of animals required to maintain a viable gene pool can be quite high, and is never known for certain. If the captive gene pool is too small, then inbreeding can result in increased susceptibility to disease, birth defects, and mutations; the species can be so weakened that it would never be viable in the wild.

Some species are extremely difficult to breed in captivity: marine mammals, many bird species, and so on. Pandas, which have been the sustained focus of captive breeding efforts for several decades in zoos around the world, are notoriously difficult to breed in captivity. With such species, the zoos, by taking animals from the wild to supply their breeding programs, constitute a net drain on wild populations.

Trouble with Reintroduction to the Wild

The whole concept of habitat restoration is mired in serious difficulties. Animals threatened by poaching (elephants, rhinos, pandas, bears and more) will never be safe in the wild as long as firearms, material needs, and a willingness to consume animal parts coincide. Species threatened by chemical contamination (such as bird species vulnerable to pesticides and lead shot) will not be candidates for release until we stop using the offending substances, and enough time has passed for the toxins to be processed out of the environment. Since heavy metals and some pesticides are both persistent and bioaccumulative, this could mean decades or centuries before it is safe to reintroduce the animal.

Even if these problems can be overcome, there are still difficulties with the process of reintroduction. Problems such as human imprinting, the need to teach animals to fly, hunt, build dens, and raise their young are serious obstacles, and must be solved individually for each species.

There is a small limit to the number of species the global network of zoos can preserve under even the most optimistic assumptions. Profound constraints are imposed by the lack of space in zoos, their limited financial resources, and the requirement that viable gene pools of each species be preserved. Few zoos, for instance, ever keep more than two individuals of large mammal species. The need to preserve scores or hundreds of a particular species would be beyond the resources of even the largest zoos, and even the whole world zoo community would be hard-pressed to preserve even a few dozen species in this manner.

Contrast this with the efficiency of large habitat preserves, which can maintain viable populations of whole complexes of species with minimal human intervention. Large preserves maintain every species in the ecosystem in a predominantly self-sufficient manner, while keeping the creatures in the natural habitat unmolested. If the financial resources (both government and charitable), and the biological expertise currently consumed by zoos, were redirected to habitat preservation and management, we would have far fewer worries about habitat restoration or preserving species whose habitat is gone.

A Question of Ethics

Choosing zoos as a means for species preservation, in addition to being expensive and of dubious effectiveness, has serious ethical

Speed Bump © 2004 Dave Coverly. Used with the permission of Dave Coverly and The Cartoonist Group.

problems. Keeping animals in zoos harms them, by denying them freedom of movement and association, which is important to social animals, and frustrates many of their natural behavioral patterns, leaving them at best bored, and at worst seriously neurotic. While humans may feel there is some justifying benefit to their captivity (that the species is being preserved, and may someday be reintroduced into the wild), this is no compensating benefit to the individual animals. Attempts to preserve species by means of captivity have been described as sacrificing the individual gorilla to the abstract Gorilla (i.e., to the abstract conception of the gorilla).

THIRTEEN

Zoos Have a Bright Future

Jeffrey P. Bonner

Zoos have a bright future ahead of them if they take several important steps, according to Jeffery Bonner, president and chief executive officer of the Saint Louis Zoo. In the face of environmental challenges and the threat of massive global extinctions, zoos must respond quickly and intelligently as catalysts for conservation. Zoos must develop their own conservation priorities, integrate them seamlessly with reintroduction into the wild, and partner with other powerful organizations and universities. Finally, zoos must push for a massive shift in public and political opinion for conservation. Without these changes, zoos stand to lose much— but with them, zoos hold profound promise for the survival of thousands of species.

The world around us is changing fast and when it comes to wildlife, it is not changing for the better. The IUCN [International Union for the Conservation of Nature] publishes the international list of threatened and endangered species (called the Red List), and a quick look at their list will tell you this: 18 percent of the world's remaining mammals and 11 percent of the world's remaining birds are threatened with extinction. As Bill Conway recently summarized, "Almost all large

Jeffrey P. Bonner, from *Sailing with Noah: Stories from the World Of Zoos*. Columbia, MO: University of Missouri Press, 2006. Copyright © 2006 by The Curators of the University of Missouri. All rights reserved. Reprinted by permission of the University of Missouri Press.

animals are in trouble; storks and cranes, pythons and crocodiles, great apes (in fact, most of the primates), elephants and rhinoceroses. Ninety percent of black rhinoceroses have been killed in the past eighteen years and one-third of the world's 266 turtle species are now threatened with extinction." Amphibians are disappearing worldwide. Add to that reports of acid rain, ozone depletion, global warming, the destruction of the world's rain forests, and phytoplankton blooms and coral bleaching in our oceans, and you get the picture of a world on the precipice of environmental disaster.

In his essay. "The Changing Role of Zoos in the 21st Century," Bill Conway quotes Jack Welch, CEO of General Electric, who once said, "When the rate of change on the outside exceeds the rate of change on the inside, the end is in sight." The problem, according to Conway, is that the "outside" world of wildlife and nature, which the world's zoos represent to millions of visitors every year, is clearly changing faster than the "internal" zoo response. In other words, zoo have got to start doing things differently. And they have to start now. We have been overtaken by the magnitude and speed of extinction. If we do not respond, the zoo of the future will be little more than a living museum.

Becoming Catalysts for Conservation

In 2004 a small group of zoo professionals from around the world gathered in London to think about precisely this problem, "How can zoos transform themselves so that they'll be able to respond, in a fundamental way, to massive global extinctions?" The conclusion of this conference was that zoos must redefine themselves in a completely different way—in the words of one zoo professional, they must become in situ conservation organizations. This means that the fundamental role of zoos, their reason for being, must become the preservation of animals in the wild. Much like Conservation International (CI) and the World Wildlife Fund [WWF], our zoos must become protectors of wildlife and wild places. But there are fundamental differences between CI and

Zoos are the center of conservation efforts with many species of animals.

WWF and zoos. Zoos have a whole different set of strengths and assets than international conservation organizations (of course, they also have some problems that the major international organizations don't have).

Zoos have several things that make them unique. First, zoo professionals are the world's experts on breeding small populations of endangered species. No other class of research or conservation organizations, universities, in fact, nobody else, has that skill set. Second, we have living things. We have an incredible variety of living things—everything from anteaters to amphibians, birds to butterflies, conger eels to capybara—I could go through the entire alphabet, but you get the idea. That is a resource no one else has. Third, zoos are already used to collaboration. We cooperate in the management of all of the animals that are in Species Survival Plans (SSPs), we collaborate on research projects, and we collaborate on field efforts like those of the Madagascar Fauna Group. Fourth, we have visitors. WWF and CI don't get the more than three million visitors a year that the Saint Louis Zoo does. That is a huge, albeit largely untapped, resource.

So these are, I think, our major strengths. We hold over ten thousand different species of animals from all parts of the world, many of them rare or endangered; we host more visitors annually than all major professional sports combined; and we have unique expertise in the management of animals, unique capabilities for research on exotic species, and a high potential for developing conservation collaborations. In the end, I believe that zoos hold extraordinary promise, perhaps the greatest promise of any type of conservation organization, for preserving wild things in wild places, providing a safety net for charismatic species in danger of extinction, and mobilizing the interests and passion of the general public for worldwide conservation. . . .

Seamless Conservation

So, first, zoos need to develop their own conservation priorities. In many cases they will overlap perfectly with the priorities of other conservation organizations, but in some cases, they will not. Second, we must reorganize ourselves internally to meet the prioritized need. This means that our collections and thus our breeding programs need to relate to our priorities. I've already mentioned that many zoos hold common zebras, even though rarest of the three species of zebras, the Grevy's zebra, is rapidly becoming extinct. That just doesn't make any sense. Zoos can be an important safety net for the Grevy's, and if they become extinct in the wild or, almost as bad, their populations become so small that they are genetically compromised, we can reintroduce animals back to the wild.

In other words, zoos have to achieve what we might call "integrated seamless conservation" from our zoo out to the wild—from inside our fence, back out to the field. The Madagascar Fauna Group [MFG] is often used as an example. We have bred lemurs in zoos, returned them to our zoo in Madagascar, allowed them to learn how to survive in the wild, and then released them back to the wild. That, in a nutshell, is integrated conservation.

Powerful Alliances

This leads me to the third thing that must happen. Zoos cannot work alone. We have to partner with organizations like CI and WWF, with universities, and with a wide variety of local conservation organizations, governmental agencies—indeed, with a vast arena of potential partners—if we are to be successful. Again, the MFG provides a pretty good example. We work with Duke University and SUNY [State University of New York]–Stony Brook very closely. Conservation International is a wonderful partner, as is the Wildlife Conservation Society. But we also work with the government of Madagascar and with two major universities in Madagascar. Nothing happens without that high degree of co-operation and collaboration. Nothing.

Fueling Support for Conservation

Finally, zoos must lead the way in pushing for a massive shift in social and political support for conservation. This means not only that we have to convince our millions upon millions of visitors that they should be interested and invested in these efforts, but also that we need to work with our government and other governments to push this agenda. Most zoo directors and zoo trustees are scared to death of doing so, but we simply have to. We must advocate for wild things and wild places, and we must use our considerable political muscle to do so. Zoo directors are getting pretty good at lobbying, but our boards are rarely, if ever, called on to help. That must change.

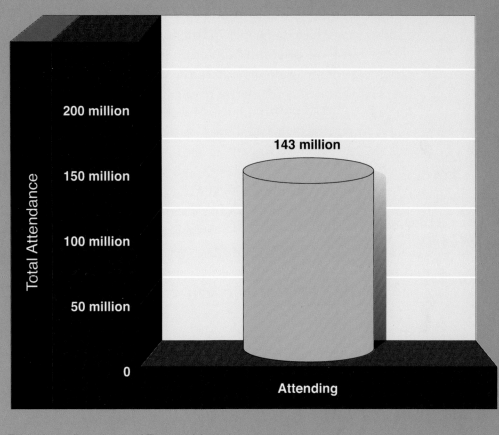

Total Attendance for All AZA-Accredited Zoos and Aquariums for 2005

200 million

143 million

150 million

Total Attendance

100 million

50 million

0

Attending

Taken from: Association of Zoos and Aquariums, 2005.

It used to be, decades ago, that we used boards primarily, in fact almost exclusively, as fund-raisers: That accounts for the customary "three Gs" of board involvement (*get* us money, *give* us money, or *get* the heck out of here). But as discussed earlier, now it's more common to think of boards in terms of the "three Ws"—we want your *wealth*, yes, but we also want your *wisdom* and we want you to *work* hard for our institutions. Perhaps now we should talk about the "three Is"—we certainly still want boards to generate *income*, but we also want them for *inspiration* and, most importantly in the emerging world of zoo conservation, we want their *influence*. The battle for saving wild things in wild places will not be fought in the field as much as it will be waged on the political front.

In short, we have to change in two profound ways. We have to change our basic orientation in order to become full and complete field conservation organizations, and we have to change in terms of what we communicate to our audience and how we utilize our vast audience to understand and influence both the social and political directions that our society takes.

FOURTEEN

Zoos Should Be Abolished

Mercy for Animals

Zoos should be abolished according to Mercy for Animals (MF), a nonprofit organization that believes nonhuman animals deserve the right to live free of unnecessary suffering. Not only are zoo animals kept in grossly inadequate conditions, they are the blameless victims of profit-maximizing business practices that do not respect their physical, mental, or physiological welfare. Zoo animals are exploited from day one, prematurely taking them from their mothers, while older, less attractive animals are euthanized or sold to exotic animal dealers to make room for "cuter" babies. In addition, zoos fail in their endeavors to educate the public and to reintroduce animals back into the wild. In short, zoos are despicable organizations and the world would be better off without them. MFA is dedicated to promoting nonviolence toward all animals through public education campaigns, demonstrations, and open rescues.

Despite their professed concern for animals, zoos remain more "collections" of interesting "items" than actual havens or simulated habitats. Zoos teach people that it is acceptable to keep animals in captivity, bored, cramped, lonely, and far from their natural homes.

Mercy for Animals, "Zoos," www.mercyforanimals.org, July 7, 2007. Reproduced by permission.

Says Virginia McKenna, star of the classic movie Born Free and now an active campaigner in behalf of captive animals: "It is the sadness of zoos which haunts me. The purposeless existence of the animals. For the four hours we spend in a zoo, the animals spend four years, or fourteen, perhaps even longer—if not in the same zoo then in others—day and night; summer and winter. . . . This is not conservation and surely it is not education. No, it is 'entertainment.' Not comedy, however, but tragedy."

Bad Zoo Conditions

Zoos range in size and quality from cageless parks to small roadside menageries with concrete slabs and iron bars. The larger the zoo and the greater the number and variety of the animals it contains, the more it costs to provide quality care for the animals. Although more than 112 million people visit zoos in the United States and Canada every year, most zoos operate at a loss and must find ways to cut costs (which sometimes means selling animals) or add gimmicks that will attract visitors. Zoo officials often consider profits ahead of the animals' well-being. A former director of the Atlanta Zoo once remarked that he was "too far removed from the animals; they're the last thing I worry about with all the other problems."

Animals suffer from more than neglect in some zoos. When Dunda, an African elephant, was transferred from the San Diego Zoo to the San Diego Wild Animal Park, she was chained, pulled to the ground, and beaten with ax handles for two days. One witness described the blows as "home run swings." Such abuse may be the norm. "You have to motivate them," says San Francisco zookeeper Paul Hunter of elephants, "and the way you do that is by beating the hell out of them."

Zoos Fail to Educate

Zoos claim to educate people and preserve species, but they frequently fall short on both counts. Most zoo enclosures are quite small, and labels provide little more information than the species'

A baby meerkat sticks close to his mother's side at the San Diego Zoo. Failure in zoo animals to thrive may point to a lack of proper care and space.

name, diet, and natural range. The animals' normal behavior is seldom discussed, much less observed, because their natural needs are seldom met. Birds' wings may be clipped so they cannot fly, aquatic animals often have little water, and the many animals who naturally live in large herds or family groups are often kept alone or, at most, in pairs. Natural hunting and mating behaviors are virtually eliminated by regulated feeding and breeding regimens. The animals are closely confined, lack privacy, and have little opportunity for mental stimulation or physical exercise, resulting in abnormal and self-destructive behavior, called zoochosis.

Unhappy Animals

A worldwide study of zoos conducted by the Born Free Foundation revealed that zoochosis is rampant in confined animals around the globe. Another study found that elephants spend 22 percent of their time engaging in abnormal behaviors, such as repeated head bobbing or biting cage bars, and bears spend about 30 percent of their time pacing, a sign of distress.

One sanctuary that is home to rescued zoo animals reports seeing frequent signs of zoochosis in animals brought to the sanctuary from zoos. Of chimpanzees, who bite their own limbs from captivity-induced stress, the manager says: "Their hands were unrecognizable from all the scar tissue."

More than half the world's zoos "are still in bad conditions" and treating chimpanzees poorly, according to renowned chimpanzee expert Jane Goodall.

Number of Species in AZA-Accredited Zoos

Type of Animal	Total Number of Individual Animals
Amphibians	14,916
Birds	57,115
Fish	339,195
Invertebrates	239,925
Mammals	53,189
Marine Mammals	1,260
Reptiles	29,573

Taken from: AZA.

As for education, zoo visitors usually spend only a few minutes at each display, seeking entertainment rather than enlightenment. A study of the zoo in Buffalo, N.Y., found that most people passed cages quickly, and described animals in such terms as "funny-looking," "dirty," or "lazy."

Failed Conservation Efforts

The purpose of most zoos' research is to find ways to breed and maintain more animals in captivity. If zoos ceased to exist, so would the need for most of their research. Protecting species from extinction sounds like a noble goal, but zoo officials usually favor exotic or popular animals who draw crowds and publicity, and neglect less popular species. Most animals housed in zoos are not endangered, nor are they being prepared for release into natural habitats. It is nearly impossible to release captive-bred animals into the wild. A 1994 report by the World Society for the Protection of Animals showed that only 1,200 zoos out of 10,000 worldwide are registered for captive breeding and wildlife conservation. Only two percent of the world's threatened or endangered species are registered in breeding programs. Those that are endangered may have their plight made worse by zoos' focus on crowd appeal. In his book *The Last Panda*, George Schaller, the scientific director of the Bronx Zoo, says zoos are actually contributing to the near-extinction of giant pandas by constantly shuttling the animals from one zoo to another for display. Inbreeding is also a problem among captive populations.

Zoo babies are great crowd-pleasers, but what happens when babies grow up? Zoos often sell or kill animals who no longer attract visitors. Deer, tigers, lions, and other animals who breed often are sometimes sold to "game" farms where hunters pay for the "privilege" of killing them; some are killed for their meat and/or hides. Other "surplus" animals may be sold to smaller, more poorly run zoos or to laboratories for experiments.

What You Should Know About Zoos and Animal Welfare

Facts About Zoos

- There are about four hundred professionally managed zoos in the United States.

- About 98 percent of Americans say they have visited a zoo once in their lifetime.

- There are two hundred organizations in the United States that are accredited by the American Association of Zoos and Aquariums (AZA).

- In 2005 the total annual attendance for all AZA-accredited zoos and aquariums was 143 million.

- In the United States any public animal exhibit must be licensed and inspected by the United States Department of Agriculture. Zoos may also require special licenses to meet the requirements of their particular locality.

- Throughout the world millions of animals are kept in more than ten thousand zoos and hundreds of circuses.

Facts About Animal Welfare and Zoos

- The AZA estimates that there are approximately twenty-four hundred animal exhibits operating under USDA license as of February 2007; fewer than 10 percent are accredited.

- According to animal rights groups, more than 60 percent of polar bears in British zoos are mentally deranged, and cubs born in zoos are twice as likely to die as those in the wild.

- In the wild, elephants roam up to 30 miles (48km) a day.

- Forty zoo elephants have died in the past thirty years because of arthritis and foot problems, according to In Defense of Animals.

- Sixty-two percent of animals in zoos suffer from foot disease, including chronic abscesses, bone infection, toe fractures, and more, according to In Defense of Animals.

Facts About Zoos and Conservation

- AZA members participate in over seven hundred cooperative conservation and management programs.

- Collectively, zoos and aquariums spent more than $70 million on conservation and research.

- In 2005, 166 AZA-accredited zoos and aquariums reported participating in 1,719 conservation, research, and education projects in ninety-seven countries or regions.

- Almost fourteen thousand employees are engaged in conservation and science research in zoos and aquariums, supported by thirty-four hundred volunteers.

- In 1993 the World Association of Zoos and Aquariums (WAZA), formerly known as the International Union of the Directors of Zoological Gardens, produced its first conservation strategy. In November 2004 WAZA adopted a new strategy that sets out the aims and mission of zoological gardens of the twenty-first century.

- There are only about 188 pandas living in captivity worldwide. Hosting giant pandas costs each zoo an average of 2.6 million dollars a year, according to *National Geographic*.

- According to recent studies, 18 percent of the world's remaining mammals and 11 percent of the world's remaining birds are threatened with extinction.

What You Should Do About Zoos and Animal Welfare

Whether or not animals should be kept in captivity is a divisive subject, with strong opinions on both sides. Many animal welfare and animal rights activists argue that wild animals should not be kept in zoos, and suffer greatly from boredom, stress, and neglect. They claim that the zoo "business" does not really care about its animals and treats them like nameless, faceless commodities. On the other side, zoo supporters argue that most zoos have extraordinarily high standards of care, and that zoos play an important role in education, conservation, and science.

How can you form an educated opinion on the issue of zoos and animal welfare? And once you've decided which side to take, what are the steps you can take to further your ideals?

Conduct Your Own Research

It is critical to find some facts on the topic of zoos and animal welfare if you are to form a valid, educated opinion. There are many books, magazine articles, Web sites, and studies devoted to the subject of zoos, so it just takes a little bit of time and dedication to find the information you need.

A great starting point is to look at the essays contained in this book, *Zoos and Animal Welfare*. You can also visit your school or local public library to find additional resources such as books, magazine articles, and scientific journals.

Another great place to search is the Internet. Simply use a search engine like Google to pull up Web sites and information. Make a list of different search terms, such as "animal rights" and "conservation" and "captivity." The more search terms you use, the greater variety of information you will find, and the more you will learn.

You can also visit the Web sites of different zoo organizations that are listed in Organizations to Contact. There you will find many articles, links, studies, fact sheets, position papers, and information pertaining to zoos and animal welfare.

You should also visit your local zoo. Take note of all the exhibits and the conditions that the animals are living in. Do the zoo animals seem active and engaged in their environment, or bored and listless? (Keep in mind that different animals are active at different times of the day, so just because an animal is sleeping or resting does not necessarily mean that it is unhappy.) Do any of the zoo animals exhibit signs of zoochosis, such as rocking, swaying, or pacing? Make notes about what you see as you walk through the zoo.

You may also be able to conduct a first-person interview. See if you can arrange to talk to a zoo keeper. Be sure to come prepared with a list of questions so you can gather the best information possible.

Review the Information

Now that you have collected all the relevant information, it is time to start identifying the main points of the debate. You may choose to organize your information in several ways, such as dividing up the "pro zoos" information and the "against zoos" research. Or you may organize the opinions and information around several important topics, such as conservation, animal welfare, and education.

Reviewing and organizing your information will enable you to discern quickly the hot points of the debate. Make a list of the most debated topics, as they will form the basis for your opinion.

Evaluate the Research

What are the different organizations and who are the individuals that support zoos? Which ones are against zoos? You will quickly find that most key organizations involving animals have strong opinions on both sides. Which side uses more facts to support their positions? Do you find their research credible? These are important questions to ask yourself as you evaluate the merits of your body of research.

It is important to look at the individuals authoring each opinion, article, or book. Do they have a lot of experience on the topic, or are they merely expressing an opinion? Take a look at their previous work, as well as the different organizations they are involved with. You will find some articles and books to be much more believable than others based on the credibility of their authors.

It is also wise to be aware of the biases that affect the opinions of different authors. For example, one would expect an executive of the Association of Zoos and Aquariums to present information validating zoos and their standards. A member of PETA, on the other hand, will be much more focused on the health and well-being of the individual animal. Rather than just accepting all of the information as fact, it is smart to read as critically as possible.

Personal Experience

The debate over zoos and animal welfare is closely tied to your moral values and how you feel about animals. Do you feel that animals have a life of their own that is of importance aside from their utility to us? If so, in what ways must this life be respected?

Your own personal experience may affect how you feel about the issue of zoos and animal welfare. Perhaps you have a fond memory of going to the zoo and learning about the different animals. Or perhaps you have had an experience with your own pet that has influenced how you feel about the issue of animal welfare.

Examine Your Personal Values, Principles, and Biases

How do you feel when you visit a zoo? What are your impressions and feelings? Do you feel strongly one way or another that it is right or wrong to keep wild animals in captivity? Examining your personal values, principles, and morals will play a large role in choosing your position on the subject.

Take Action

Once you have conducted your own research, reviewed the information, evaluated the arguments, and examined your personal values, you will be able to form a position and take action. Not only will you be able to defend your opinion accurately, but you will be able to present compelling information either for or against zoos. You may feel very strongly one way or another, which is fine, as long as you have facts and timely, relevant data to back up your case. You may also conclude that arguments for both sides are very strong, and you are unable to take a pro-con stance. Such a decision is fair and acceptable, but you might also want to try to research a little more to see if you are swayed one way or another. Just remember that there are no wrong opinions or positions to take, as long as you back it up with good evidence.

You may feel inclined to be vocal about the position you take and promote it through various activities. Perhaps you will want to volunteer as a docent at your local zoo, or participate in animal rights meetings and campaigns to change or alter zoo practices. You may even want to join and play an active role in an organization. One of the easiest ways to be active is to share your opinion with friends and family. You can do this on an informal level, through casual discussions or e-mails, and even elicit opinions of others. You might also want to write to your local council members or congressional representatives or submit an opinion letter to your local paper. All of these are acceptable ways to take an active role. No matter what action you take, after you have gone through the process of conducting your own research, evaluating the information, examining your morals and values, and choosing a position, you will be able to discuss and defend your opinion intelligently.

ORGANIZATIONS TO CONTACT

The editors have compiled the following list of organizations concerned with the issues debated in this book. The descriptions are derived from materials provided by the organizations. All have publications or information available for interested readers. The list was compiled on the date of publication of the present volume; the information provided here may change. Be aware that many organizations take several weeks or longer to respond to inquiries, so allow as much time as possible.

Animal Welfare Institute (AWI)
PO Box 3650, Washington, DC 20027
(703) 836-4300
e-mail: awi@awionline.org
Web site: www.awionline.org

The Animal Welfare Institute is a nonprofit charitable organization founded in 1951 to reduce the sum total of pain and fear inflicted on animals by humans. In the organization's early years the emphasis was on the desperate needs of animals used for experimentation. In the decades that followed, the organization expanded the scope to address many other areas of animal suffering.

Association of Zoos and Aquariums (AZA)
8403 Colesville Rd., Suite 710, Silver Spring, MD 20910-3314
(301) 562-0777; fax: (301) 562-0888
Web site: www.aza.org

Founded in 1924, the Association of Zoos and Aquariums is a nonprofit organization dedicated to the advancement of zoos and aquariums in the areas of conservation, education, science, and recreation.

Born Free Foundation
3 Grove House, Foundry Lane, Horsham, West Sussex, RH13 5PL, UK
01403 240 170
e-mail: info@bornfree.org.uk
Web site: www.bornfree.org.uk

The Born Free Foundation is a dynamic international wildlife charity, devoted to compassionate conservation and animal welfare. Born Free takes action worldwide to protect threatened species and stop individual animal suffering. Born Free believes wildlife belongs in the wild and works to phase out zoos.

The Captive Animals' Protection Society (CAPS)
PO Box 4186, Manchester, M60 3ZA, UK
phone/fax 0845 330 3911
e-mail: info@captiveanimals.org
Web site: www.captiveanimals.org

The Captive Animals' Protection Society was established in 1957. Founder Irene Heaton was appalled by the suffering of animals within the entertainment industry, and she campaigned tirelessly on their behalf throughout the rest of her life. It is through her efforts and the influence and hard work of her successors that CAPS can be recognized today as one of this country's leading campaigning organizations on behalf of animals in circuses, zoos, and the entertainment industry.

The Humane Society of the United States (HSUS)
2100 L St. NW, Washington, DC 20037
(202) 452-1100
Web site: www.hsus.org

The Humane Society of the United States has worked since 1954 to promote the protection of all animals. With nearly 10 million members and constituents, the HSUS is the nation's largest and most powerful animal protection organization, working in the United States and abroad to defend the interests of animals. They celebrate the human-animal bond, and fight animal cruelty and abuse in all of its forms.

In Defense of Animals (IDA)
3010 Kerner Blvd., San Rafael, CA 94901
(415) 388-9641; fax: 415-388-0388
e-mail: idainfo@idausa.org

In Defense of Animals is an international animal protection organization dedicated to ending the exploitation and abuse of animals by raising the status of animals beyond that of mere property and by defending their rights, welfare, and habitat. IDA's efforts include educational events, cruelty investigation, boycotts, grassroots activism, and hands-on rescue through sanctuaries in Mississippi and Cameroon, Africa.

Mercy for Animals
3712 N. Broadway, Suite 560, Chicago, IL 60613
(866) 632-6446
e-mail: info@mercyforanimals.org
Web site: www.mercyforanimals.org

Mercy for Animals is a nonprofit animal advocacy organization that believes nonhuman animals are irreplaceable individuals with morally significant interests and hence rights, including the right to live free of unnecessary suffering. Founded in 1999, MFA is dedicated to establishing and defending the rights of all animals.

People for the Ethical Treatment of Animals (PETA)
501 Front St., Norfolk, VA 23510
(757) 622-7382
e-mail: info@peta.org
Web site: www.peta.org

People for the Ethical Treatment of Animals, with more than 1.6 million members and supporters, is the largest animal rights organization in the world. PETA focuses its attention on the four areas in which the largest numbers of animals suffer the most intensely for the longest periods of time: on factory farms, in laboratories, in the clothing trade, and in the entertainment industry. PETA works through public education, cruelty investigations, research, animal rescue, legislation, special events, celebrity involvement, and protest campaigns.

Wildlife Conservation Society (WCS)
2300 Southern Blvd., Bronx, NY 10460
(718) 220-5100
e-mail: membership@wcs.org
Web site: www.wcs.org

The Wildlife Conservation Society saves wildlife and wild lands through careful science, international conservation, education, and the management of the world's largest system of urban wildlife parks. Together, these activities change individual attitudes toward nature and help people imagine wildlife and humans living in sustainable interaction on both a local and a global scale.

Zoocheck
2646 St. Clair Ave. E., Toronto, ON, M4B 3M1, Canada
(416) 285-1744; (416) 285-4670
e-mail: info@zoocheck.com
Web site: www.zoocheck.com

Zoocheck Canada is a national animal protection charity established in 1984 to promote and protect the interests and well-being of wild animals. For more than twenty years, Zoocheck has been a leading voice for the protection of wild animals. Zoocheck is the only Canadian organization with a specific focus on captive wild animal issues and problems.

BIBLIOGRAPHY

Books

Bartay, Eric, and Hardouin-Fugier, Elisabeth, *Zoo: A History of Zoological Gardens in the West*. London: Reaktion, 2004.

Demello, Margo, and Williams, Erin, *Why Animals Matter: The Case for Animal Protection*. New York: Prometheus, 2007.

Hanson, Elizabeth, *Animal Attractions: Nature on Display in American Zoos*, New Jersey: Princeton University Press, 2004.

Nussbaum, Martha, and Sunstein, Cass, *Animal Rights: Current Debates and New Directions*. Oxford, UK: Oxford University Press, 2005.

Regan, Tom, *The Case for Animal Rights*. Berkeley and Los Angeles: University of California Press, 2004.

Rothfels, Nigel, *Savages and Beasts: The Birth of the Modern Zoo*. Baltimore: Johns Hopkins University Press, 2002.

Singer, Peter, *In Defense of Animals: The Second Wave*. Oxford, UK: Blackwell, 2005.

Workman, Dave, *Animal Rights: The Dark Side of the Animal Rights Movement*. Bellevue, Washington: Merril, 2005.

Periodicals

Francione, Gary, "One Right for All," *New Scientist*, October 8, 2005.

Guthrie, Julian, "Uproar over the Internet Market for Zoo Animals," *San Francisco Chronicle*, February 23, 2003.

Hampp, Andrew, "Animal Attraction: Marketing at the Zoo," *Advertising Age*, October 20, 2006.

Huxley, John, "Cooperation Is the Law of the Jungle, Zoos Insist," *Sydney Morning Herald*, September 2006.

Keaggy, Diane Toroian, "Herd in St. Louis Is Part of Debate on Zoo Elephants," *St. Louis Post-Dispatch*, May 21, 2006.

Lacey, Marc, "A Kenya Plan to Ship Game to Thailand Meets Protests," *New York Times*, January 25, 2005.

Laidman, Jenni, "Zoos Using Drugs to Help Manage Anxious Animals," *Toledo Blade*, September 2005.

Lemonick, Michael, "Who Belongs at the Zoo?" *Time*, June 11, 2006.

Newman, Berry, "Zoo Confinement Gives Elephants Problem Feet," *Wall Street Journal*, November 17, 2006.

Paulson, Amanda, "It's No Longer a (Traditional) Zoo Out There," *Christian Science Monitor*, June 2004.

Ross, S.R., Lonsdorf, E.V., and Stoinski, T.S., "Assessing the Welfare Implications of Visitors in a Zoo Setting," *Applied Animal Behavior Science*, 2005.

Springen, Karen, "Zoos High-Sky Birds Eye," *Newsweek*, December 12, 2006.

Stern, Andrew, "Elephant Deaths Spur New Debate Over U.S. Zoos," *Reuters*, 2005.

Weir, Kirstin, "Home Alone: What Should Alaska Do with Its Only Elephant?" *Current Science*, April 5, 2005.

Web Sites

The Good Zoo Guide Online (www.goodzoos.com). The only Web site that aims to provide official descriptions of every good zoo, wildlife park, and animal collection on the planet, as well as reviews and comments from visitors.

Help Elephants in Zoos (www.helpelephants.com). This Web site campaigns to remove animals from captivity and features news articles, expert declarations, literature, and other resources.

Society and Animals Forum (www.psyeta.org). Contains links about human-animal studies, animal education, animal welfare, and other topics.

Wildlife Pimps (www.wildlifepimps.com). This anti-zoo Web site features fact sheets, pictures, research, and campaigns dedicated to keeping animals out of captivity. This site is run by PETA, People for the Ethical Treatment of Animals.

Zoos Worldwide (www.zoos-worldwide.de). This Web site features a comprehensive list of zoos and aquariums around the world. It includes zoo cams and other links.

INDEX

PICTURE CREDITS